Post-War French Catholic
Antisemitism

Juan H. Mellen

ABSTRACT

In February 1944, Dr. Fritz and Anni Finaly, Jewish Austrians who had fled the Nazi regime for France in 1939, made a desperate decision. To protect their sons Robert and Gérald from persecution, they placed them in the care of others. The boys were eventually confined to a municipal nursery run by Antoinette Brun in Grenoble, France. After the war, Brun's refusal to return the children to their relatives led to protracted court proceedings, rendering what came to be called the Finaly Affair, the most highly publicized post-war custody case in France. This thesis will analyze how the press coverage of the guardianship, baptism, and abductions of the Finaly brothers bolstered the interests of Catholics and Jews alike. I will illustrate how the press became a key element in disseminating new forms of post-war antisemitism involving the Catholic Church and its doctrine. The coverage also promoted early and subtle forms of Holocaust memory on behalf of its Jewish victims. Jews and supporters of the Finaly children's restitution evoked memories of the Holocaust while leveraging the press as a platform to state their positions. My analysis reveals that French Jews did not remain silent about the events of the Holocaust in the early post-war years.

TABLE OF CONTENTS

LIST OF FIGURES

LIST OF ABBREVIATIONS

AFP	French Press Agency (Agence-France-Presse)
CNAL	National Committee for Secular Action (Comité national d'action laïque)
COSOR	Social Aid Committee for Resistance Organizations (Comité des œuvres sociales des organisations de Résistance)
FSJF	Federation of Jewish Societies of France (Fédération des sociétés juives de France)
JDC	Joint Distribution Committee
LICA	International League against Racism and Anti-Semitism (La Ligue International Contre Le Racisme et L'antisémitisme)
OOIG	Organization for Jewish War Orphans (Œuvre des Orphelins Israélites de Guerre)
OSE	Children's Relief Agency (Œuvre de secours aux enfants)
PSF	French Social Party Parti Social Français
UJRE	Union of Jews for Resistance and Mutual Aid (Union des juifs pour la résistance et l'entraide)
UNADIF	National Union of Associations of Deportees and Internees of the Resistance and Families (Union Nationale des Associations de Déportés et Internés de la Résistance et Familles)

Introduction

On February 10, 1944, Dr. Fritz and Anni Finaly, Jewish Austrians who had fled the Nazi regime for France in 1939, made a desperate decision. To protect their children from persecution, they placed their sons Robert and Gérald, then nearly three and one-year old, first in a children's home and days later with a family friend after the director of the children's home fled for her life. Because of their young ages, Robert and Gérald were eventually confined to a nursery run by Antoinette Brun in Grenoble. Unlike the overwhelming majority of the general population, Mademoiselle Brun undertook considerable risk to save Robert, Gérald, and possibly seven other Jewish children from Nazi persecution.[2] She can thus be counted among the small number of institutions and individuals who bravely rescued 8,000 to 10,000 Jewish children in France during World War II.[3] However, in 1948 she undertook a less laudable act: upon her initiative, Brun had Robert and Gérald baptized despite full knowledge that their biological family was seeking their return. By imposing her religious beliefs on the lives of two little boys after the war, she replaced Jewish children with "Christian" children and thus helped perpetuate the eradication of Jewish culture that the Nazis had begun.

Brun's unwillingness to return the children led to protracted and sensationalized court proceedings, rendering what came to be called the Finaly Affair the most highly publicized post-war custody case in France. Although Hedwig Rosner, the boys' aunt, was ultimately granted legal guardianship of Robert and Gérald in 1952, taking them into her care in 1953, this outcome came only after an elaborate deception was undertaken by Brun and the Catholic Church, who conspired to hide the boys often under false names.

While a number of scholars have already addressed the events surrounding the Finaly Affair, they have overlooked how newspaper coverage of the guardianship, baptism, and abductions of Robert and Gérald Finaly bolstered the interests of Catholics and Jews alike. I argue that it became a key element in disseminating new forms of post-war antisemitism involving the Catholic Church and its doctrine as well as promoting early and subtle forms of Holocaust memory on behalf of its Jewish victims. On the one hand, the press provided the Church and its faithful with a platform to promote its interests, many of which were rooted in historic antisemitism. These reflected a new and more subtle way to put Jews and Jewish organizations on the defensive while maintaining a public face of benevolence toward Jews. At the same time, the press's promotion of the views of Jewish individuals and groups helped disseminate early and subtle forms of Holocaust memory that may have helped bolster the case for the children's return to their family.

While this thesis draws upon a variety of sources, including archival evidence from the Moshe Keller Collection at Yad Vashem, the foundation of my analysis will be press coverage of the Finaly Affair in general, and coverage of it by *Le Monde* in particular. As France's newspaper of record, *Le Monde* has high journalistic standards, is known for exceptional coverage of events and has a high global circulation.[4] In the spring of 1953, the diversity of opinion on the case played out in the pages of *Le Monde* as well as other publications. This work will add to existing scholarship, which has not specifically analyzed *Le Monde*'s coverage of the Finaly Affair as a window to the post-war existence and perpetuation of antisemitism by Catholic clergy and lay people who refused to return Jewish children to the custody of their relatives because they had been "saved" through Catholic baptism. Current scholarship also lacks recognition of the ways in which the coverage of the Finaly Affair helped form a basis for early forms of Holocaust memory, showing that Jews and others did not remain silent about the genocide of the Jews in these early post-war years and providing a platform for those seeking to have the children returned.

Prior to expounding on the antisemitism which surfaced during one of the most high-profile custody cases of the post-war period, it is necessary to gain a foundational understanding of events. First, I will elaborate on the circumstances which determined the entrustment of Robert and Gérald Finaly to Antoinette Brun, the Directrice of Grenoble's municipal nursery. Brun's duplicitous attitude as well as her contribution to a long and agonizing legal battle will be introduced. Key dates and facts will be cited with regard to the children's baptism, abductions and return. A brief foundation will be laid down on the topic of Jewish orphans who remained in Catholic custody in post-war France as well as the humanitarian organizations which helped to reunite them with their families. The Finaly family was no exception in this regard and accepted the support of several organizations in their quest to reclaim Robert and Gérald.

Existing scholarship will be briefly acknowledged prior to a more targeted discussion on *Le Monde* in section two. I will explore the origin of the newspaper as a free and independent publication and its placement on the political spectrum as compared to other French publications of the era. *Le Monde*'s editorial approach will be examined, which included a substantial use of special correspondents, external contributors and the republication of articles from other newspapers. This background will provide a basis for a wider examination of the role the press played in perpetuating antisemitic ideas in the context of the Finaly Affair. The scholarly debate about the "silence" of French Jews with regard to Jewish matters, particularly the Holocaust in the post-war period, will be defined. Revealing that both Jews and non-Jews did not remain silent, as it pertained to the Finaly Affair, my analysis marks an early form of Holocaust memory.

Guardianship in the Finaly Affair and the pervasiveness of historical Catholic antisemitism in its new, post-war iteration will be the focus of section three. A brief background of historical Catholic antisemitism will be provided to support the understanding of how and where antisemitism surfaced in the case. Catholicism, as it was in 1953, will also be examined to provide context on how the faith and its followers were different from the Catholicism and Catholics of today. Specific to Antoinette Brun, this thesis will examine her attitude and her actions. By using archival evidence as well as secondary sources, Brun's antisemitic actions as well as her intentions with the children will be illuminated. Following this, I will analyze the range of representations of Brun in the press, specifically looking at articles written by her supporters and those written by her admonishers. These articles also illustrate Brun's own self-narrative, in which she contributed to the perpetuation of antisemitism by portraying herself as a hero, a victim, or a martyr depending on her audience.

Why did Catholic baptism dramatically change the stakes with regard to the Finaly Affair? This will be the focus of section four. After providing a brief foundation on the sacrament, I will further explore how Catholic baptism, when administered to Jewish children by force, contributes to an erasure of Jewish culture. I will also highlight how baptism and

Church doctrine relied on the separation of baptized children from all Jewish influence. In this way Church doctrine provided justification for familial separation. The press debate, specific to the Finaly Affair and baptism, will be examined from both sides. While the press outwardly projected a benevolence toward the Jews, it allowed a platform for conservative and Catholic responses, which put Jews and Jewish organizations on the defensive and triggered impassioned rebuttals.

Ritual abduction is at the heart of section five. The historical precedence for the Church's abduction of Jewish children will be shown by looking at two nineteenth century cases. Turning to the abductions in the Finaly Affair, we will examine the wide support for the imprisoned clergy and Catholic lay people as well as the debate between civil and divine law. We will attempt to ascertain how the strict adherence to doctrine could justify kidnapping and abductions, acts considered by most to be reprehensible.

The final section aims to provide a larger understanding of the motivations of Chief Rabbi Kaplan and the Catholic Church to negotiate for an agreement for the return of the children. The conclusion will provide the key findings of this analysis, specifically how the newspaper coverage, during the Finaly Affair, perpetuated antisemitism in its reports of the guardianship, baptism, and abductions of Robert and Gérald Finaly. The progress of Judeo-Catholic relations, in light of the Finaly case, will be introduced as an area of future study.

The Events of the Finaly Affair

Robert and Gérald Finaly were born on April 14, 1941, and June 3, 1942, making them nearly three and one-year old when their parents made their fateful decision in the winter of

1944. Shortly after the Finaly children were entrusted to the Saint-Vincent-de-Paul children's home in Meylan, not far from where the family lived in Grenoble, Anne-Marie Fabin, the owner and director, fled for fear of her own life. The Finaly parents then entrusted the boys to family friend Marie Poupaert. Dr. Fritz and Anni Finaly were arrested by the Gestapo on February 14, 1944, and deported to Drancy. On March 7, 1944, they were transferred to Auschwitz in a convoy and would never return. Poupaert, anxious about the situation, attempted to place the boys at the Notre-Dame de Sion convent in Grenoble, a religious order founded with the mission to convert Jews. Because of their youth, the convent recommended that the boys be placed at the municipal nursery run by Antoinette Brun. Brun claimed to have already hidden seven Jewish children at the Château de Vif. There is doubt as to whether this was true.[5] Robert and Gérald would remain at the château until the end of 1945.[6]

After the war, Robert and Gérald's aunts and uncles became aware of the children's survival and placement with Mademoiselle Brun. Margaret Fischl, the boys' aunt in New Zealand, was the first family member to pursue custody of the children. On May 15, 1945, Fischl requested immigration permits for the children's travel to New Zealand. Additionally, Fischl wrote to Antoinette Brun to express her gratitude and her desire to obtain custody of her nephews.[7] On September 12, 1945, Fischl wrote to Marie Poupaert hoping that Brun understood her intentions to take custody of the children, which was her own desire as well as the desire of her deceased brother and sister-in-law. She wrote, "I'd like to have the boys come to the 'New Zealand House' as soon as possible ... we are waiting for the permission of the French authorities for their departure. Please share this letter with Mademoiselle Brun. To this day, I can hardly believe that I have lost two brothers and my sister-in-law."[8] This example illustrates Fischl's strong desire to be reunited with her nephews as well as the pain of loss that she had already experienced. The letter also hints at anxiety within the Jewish community about children who remained in the custody of non-Jews after the war.

Initially, the family attempted to regain legal custody of Robert and Gérald without litigation. Their efforts to contact Antoinette Brun resulted in disappointment. In 1948, Margaret Fischl attempted to resolve the issue through the Roman Catholic Church, which only solidified Antoinette Brun's opposition to returning the children. At the same time, Hedwig Rosner, the boys' aunt in Israel, engaged Moshe Keller as the family's representative in Grenoble. When Keller contacted Brun, she not only refused to return the children: she declared that she had had the children baptized Catholic.[9]

Antoinette Brun's actions included numerous appeals, demands for provisional release and outright evasion of the law. These actions lengthened an agonizing and emotional legislative battle. The case included four rounds of family court proceedings starting on January 7, 1949 and continuing until July, 1952. The third proceeding, in August 1949, determined that the children should be entrusted to Hedwig Rosner or the family's agent without delay. Brun refused to comply and on August 9, filed a complaint appealing on the grounds of procedural irregularity. The next day the civil court annulled the decision of the third family counsel on the basis that the Justice of the Peace was incompetent.

In early June, 1950, the civil court of Grenoble declared the official deaths of Dr. Fritz and Anni Finaly to have been on March 7, 1944. In France, children whose parents were deported were officially under the provisional guardianship of the Departmental Offices of Veterans Affairs. Because their parents' deaths were officially declared, Robert and Gérald

Finaly would benefit from provisions awarded to war orphans under an ordinance from April 25, 1945.[10] This declaration would have implications in the outcome of the trial. Several months later, the fourth family court proceeding began on November 14, 1950 and would last until December 5. The aunts and uncles Finaly were represented by their designated agents with the exception of Otto Schwarz who remained in Austria. Antoinette Brun was not represented. In Brun's absence, Rosner was again named the guardian. On December 15, 1950, Moshe Keller requested an ordinance obligating Mademoiselle Brun to turn over the children within twenty-four hours. To this, Brun demanded the annulment of the decision of the fourth family court decision on the basis that Otto Schwarz was not represented.[11] The final legal decision was issued by the court of appeals on June 11, 1952, designating Rosner as the children's legal guardian. However, a few days later, when Moshe Keller and the bailiff went to Brun's home to collect the children, they had disappeared. Rather than return them, Antoinette Brun and members of the clergy evaded French law, secretly moving Robert and Gérald between Catholic institutions. This act represented the first abduction of Robert and Gérald Finaly.

The boys' most fraught disappearance occurred on February 3, 1953, when the children disappeared from their Bayonne dormitory in the early morning. In collusion with other religious and lay people, two abbots paid 30,000 francs ($8500 US in 1953) for the children to be guided illegally over the Pyrenees to Spain and 10,000 francs ($3000 US in 1953) to outfit them for the mountain passage. The children would not be seen publicly until June of the same year. The ensuing media frenzy and its negative reflection on the Church finally led Roman Catholic officials to propose the children's return, a decision approved by Pope Pius XII on March 23, 1953. Concurrently, there was a separate negotiation for the children's return, referred to as the agreement of March 6. The Finaly family, Chief Rabbi Jacob Kaplan of the

Central Consistory, Cardinal Pierre-Marie Gerlier, the Archbishop of Lyon, and the Social Aid

Committee for Resistance Organizations (COSOR), a French government organization tasked

with supporting deportees and their families, made a cooperative attempt to facilitate the

return of the children. After numerous delays, rumors and fears that the children were in poor

health or even dead, the children returned to France, crossing the international bridge in

Hendaye. In late July, the Finaly brothers flew to Israel with their Aunt Hedwig where they

would make their lives. When they traveled to Israel, Robert was 12 and Gérald 11.

Jewish Orphans in Post-war France

During World War II, entire families were separated and destroyed, leaving children

without a support network. In 1944, it was estimated that 5,000 to 10,000 Jewish orphans

needed care. [12] Institutions and families rescued an estimated 8,000 to 10,000 Jewish children

from Nazi persecution.[13] After the war, Jewish organizations claimed that 3,000 children

remained hidden in France, Holland and Belgium in non-Jewish families or institutions. There

was a marked anxiety amongst Jews and Jewish organizations with regard to children who

remained in the custody of non-Jews after the Liberation, particularly since many were

considered to be at risk of being converted.[14]

After the war, Jewish children came to represent the future of Judaism and provided a

subject on which to articulate an early form of Holocaust memory.[15] In a meeting with Pope

Pius XII in March 1946, Issac Halevi Herzog, Chief Rabbi of Palestine, broached the issue of

Jewish children who remained in Catholic custody. Rabbi Herzog first thanked the Pope for the

Jewish lives, which were saved by Catholics during the war. With regard to Jewish children who were still in Catholic custody, he expressed the unacceptability that Jewish children remained "cut off from their origins." Herzog added that "every child for us signifies one thousand children."[16] Echoing this anxiety, during a speaking engagement, Myriam Kubowitzki, wife of the US Secretary General of the World Jewish Congress, told the audience that "our people lost too much in this war, and children, for every people, represent the most precious treasure." Kubowitzki added that many of the children "are in Catholic convents. We have to take them out of this environment as soon as possible, even if they have no food and clothes."[17] At the heart of this anxiety was the fear that non-Jewish guardianship would result in an erasure of Jewish culture, which was especially precarious after the Holocaust.

Jewish organizations as well as relatives scoured French cities and the countryside for Jewish children who had been hidden from the Nazis. They proclaimed that the children's "estrangement from the Jewish community represented Nazi genocide by another means."[18] There was no single process for tabulating the number of orphaned children in custody, especially those who were hidden, after the war. The numbers that were estimated by the groups varied widely.[19] The Oeuvre de secours aux enfants (OSE), a Jewish relief organization, regularly visited these children and by the end of 1945 the OSE had opened twenty-five establishments in France.[20] Although there was an expectation among French authorities and the public that the state would financially participate in the efforts to restitute the children, the Joint Distribution Committee (JDC), the primary American Jewish humanitarian organization, subsidized 60% of the costs. From 1945 through 1948, Jewish Americans sent $194 million dollars to Europe through the JDC. France held a place of privilege in their efforts because when compared to countries like Belgium and Holland, France had a higher survival rate numbering

182,000 to 200,000 individuals. In the decade following the war, $27 million was sent to French Jews by American Jewish Organizations. This support came to be referred to as the "Jewish Marshall Plan." The term was first used in the 1990s by JDC leader Ralph Goldman to talk about the American Jewish initiative to reconstruct post-Holocaust European Jewish life.[21]

Jewish humanitarian organizations formed an important source of support for the Finaly family in their efforts to rehome Gérald and Robert. On July 19, 1946, Margaret Fischl, the children's aunt in New Zealand, addressed a telegram to both the OSE and her sister-in-law Augusta, asking them to inquire about the children. On October 25, 1946, Augusta made a trip to Grenoble. Her first stop was the OSE branch to request their help in convincing Antoinette Brun to return the children. A social assistant from the OSE, who already knew Robert and Gérald, was assigned to Augusta. Together they bought toys for the children with the anticipation of seeing them.[22] When they arrived at Brun's door and stated their intention to reclaim the children, Brun replied that "the Jews are not grateful" and that they did not appreciate her sacrifice. Brun also stated, "Let it be known, I will never return the children." Augusta and the OSE representative did end up seeing Robert and Gérald, presumably at the Château de Vif, where they gave the children the toys that they purchased. This is relevant because when Augusta later went to the OSE branch in Paris, she learned that Brun had complained about the visit, indicating that they had not brought anything for the children. Augusta would remark that it was fortunate to have an OSE representative with her to witness Brun's behavior.[23]

While continuing to receive support from the OSE, the family realized that they needed additional support. In September 1948, the Joint Distribution Committee (JDC), also known as

"The Joint," agreed to subsidize all of the legal expenses as well as the personal expenses of Moshe Keller, the family's representative in France.[24] Additionally, the Organization for Jewish War Orphans (OOIG), the public representative for Jewish child welfare organizations on custody disputes, was actively monitoring the case.[25] COSOR, an organization that supported deportees and their families, also would assist with the negotiations between the Finaly family, the Church and Chief Rabbi Kaplan of the Central Consistory for the return of the children. The Central Consistory was established in 1808 between the French state and French Jews to facilitate cooperation and centralize Jewish life. After 1905, the Consistory ceased to exist as an official public organization. It continued to maintain its role, albeit symbolically, to represent the Jews of France.[26]

In order to understand the motivation to not want to return a child to their family, it is important to understand some of the sentiments which existed in post-war France. These viewpoints influenced the views on how children, particularly Jewish orphans, should be raised. There were competing views primarily from those who adhered to laïcité or secularism and French republican ideals. French republicanism included the belief in a united, democratic and secular France. Another belief is that all citizens are equal before the law and no one person or part of the French population can exercise sovereignty over French citizens as a whole. French Republicanism guarantees the freedom of religion and includes the belief that no one should be forced to respect religious dogma. Founded on the separation of religion and state, France assumes a neutral stance toward all religion.[27] Since all French citizens are considered to be on an equal plane, specific community experiences and identities can be obstructed or overlooked. In the case of Jewish orphans in post-war France, this ignorance of difference was a particular form of antisemitism which did not acknowledge the Jewishness of children or interests of the Jewish community. Some non-Jews also accused Jewish humanitarian organizations of privileging sectarian politics over the needs of the child.[28] It was common that non-Jewish individuals and agencies believed that, when all was said and done, a loving family served the best interest of the child. They preferred to maintain the family structures which were forged during the war.[29] The influence of French republicanism led citizens, especially those who rescued or fostered Jewish children to see the children not as a foreign element but as a way to rebuild the population of France.[30] Non-Jews, by viewing the children in a way that might be described as "colorblind," accepted the children into their own families, while disregarding the feelings and desires of the Jewish families who sought to reclaim them. These non-Jewish families, by retaining the children, contributed to an erasure of Jewish culture.

The Jewish community, in the aftermath of the Holocaust, began to reevaluate the notion of family and look toward collective approaches, which included "colonies de vacances" (sleep-away camps), children's homes and kibbutzim. Providing children with Jewish culture and Jewish identity was of the highest importance to the community. Even children who reunited with their parents would spend time in collective settings to gain more exposure to their heritage. At the same time, European politicians and influencers felt strongly that the nuclear family structure was a way to forge stability and promote democracy. They associated collective approaches with the Nazis and their interventions into family life.[31] This association represented yet another reason to justify not returning a Jewish child to their family or to a Jewish organization.

The press also provided examples of reluctance to support the reunions of Jewish orphans with their surviving family members. *Liberation,* a newspaper leaning to the left of center with origins in the French resistance, published a series by Alexis Danan, which was severely unsympathetic to Jewish parents who were attempting to reclaim their children. Danan argued that while "these children might dream of a mother they idealize…in reality they truly do not wish to find her again." Danan went on to say, "that the most astute among them … actually wish, on the contrary, never to find her again. [32] His message was that the children's new environment had already absorbed them, and their current parents were capable of fulfilling all of their needs. Danan, himself an advocate for adoption, and *Liberation,* which provided him with an unmediated platform, illustrate the latent antisemitism in France at the time. [33]

While French republican views were common in the post-war period, they did not preclude opinions that were more in line with traditional Catholicism which were also latently antisemitic. [34] These more traditional viewpoints included strict adherence to Catholic doctrine often at the expense or in disregard of non-Catholics and a belief in the superiority of divine law over civil law. These views will be elaborated on throughout this thesis.

Existing Scholarship

Existing academic work touches on the media coverage of the case but tends to analyze it through a variety of publications. Priscilla Dale Jones published an analysis of the Finaly case in her article "The Finaly Affair: Issues and Implications" (1983). Jones' coverage of *Le Monde* focuses on three open letters written by Paul Benichou, a French Algerian Jew and intellectual, Abbot André Deroo, a Catholic priest and writer, and Rabbi Jais of the Central Consistory in Paris, representing the secular, Catholic and Jewish views respectfully. From these sources,

Jones took up the themes of the centrality of Catholic baptism and nature of the sacraments,

civil law versus divine law, anticlericalism and antisemitism.[35] *Les Enfants Cachés: L'Affaire*

Finaly (2006), by Catherine Poujol, is a comprehensive analysis of the Finaly Affair. At this time,

Catherine Poujol is the preeminent scholar on the Finaly Affair and *Les Enfants Cachés: L'Affaire*

Finaly is necessary reading material on the subject. Poujol has focused on the media coverage

and the issues that it raised in 1953. She has also used archival sources to analyze open

questions and theories about the case. The opening of Pope Pius XII's Apostolic Archive in 2020

elicited new information about the Vatican's involvement in post-war child custody cases and

provides additional context on the Finaly Affair. Significantly, as David Kertzer has shown, there

is evidence which provides a fuller picture of the antisemitic sentiments at the Vatican in the

post-war period. For example, Monsignor Angelo Dell'Acqua, entrusted by the pope as the

Secretary of State's expert on all Jewish questions, had strong antisemitic views. The pope

approved many of Dell'Acqua's suggestions with regard to the custody of Jewish children and in

particular the Finaly case. While both Poujol and Kertzer explore antisemitism in the Finaly

Affair, there is room to delve further on the topic of historic Roman Catholic antisemitism,

which includes Catholic supersessionism and abduction, antisemitic assumptions about "Jews,"

anti-Zionist tendencies, and the future of Catholic-Jewish dialogue.

Le Monde: A Balanced Perspective?

History

Le Monde was founded on December 19, 1944 by Hubert Beuve-Méry at the request of

Charles de Gaulle. Beuve-Méry described himself as having entirely "Breton ancestry" and

having grown up "immersed in the Church." Beuve-Méry is known to have said that "Breton heritage, a source of pride, and Catholicism are intimately linked." Despite his ascent into the

Bourgeoisie, he was not born with wealth. He was taken in by the Church at a young age and

educated by its institutions.[36] Regardless of Beuve-Méry's Catholic heritage, *Le Monde's*

coverage remained fairly independent. *Le Monde* was created as a national free press to

replace *Le Temps* which was France's newspaper of record from 1861 until 1942. *Le Temps* had

suffered from corruption. The newspaper, assumed to provide factual news, was subsidized by

multiple foreign governments. In 1939 the newspaper described Hitler as a brave man who

liked peace. In Beuve-Méry's own words:

> For me, the legacy of *Le Temps* is what I learned there about venality. What I experienced in my youth,
> between 1928 and 1939, was simply abominable ... I saw representatives from almost all French
> newspapers passing through Central Europe: They embodied the most blatant corruption ...

According to historian Jacque Tibau, *Le Temps* "self-destructed" on November 19, 1942, just

three days after the Germans entered the free zone. *Le Temps*, once followed by intellectuals

and elites, "had not met the challenge of the great crisis of the thirties, the rise of Nazism, the

defeat and the occupation ... it had, in its domain contributed to the disaster of 1940" and was

erased from the French journalistic milieu.[37]

Le Monde was founded to be a free and independent press and its overarching goal was

to provide information. Catherine Poujol chose *Le Monde* for her research on the Finaly Affair

because it was "remarkably neutral" and aimed above all at providing information. Poujol

argues that *Le Monde* differed from the press of the era, which was more of an opinion press.[38]

As France's newspaper of record, it would have subjected its journalists to additional rigor and

fact checking, which is perceivable in the coverage of the Finaly case. I do not agree that *Le

Monde* was neutral. Unlike other newspapers of the time, *Le Monde*'s coverage was less sensational, although not entirely neutral. It is evident from analyzing the over 150 articles that *Le Monde* published on the Finaly Affair from January to July of 1953, that their coverage leaned toward the left. Despite director Hubert Beuve-Mery's Catholic background, the commentary and editorials indicate an anticlerical bias and a suspicion of the Church's role in the abduction. Overall, the paper supported the return of the Finaly children to their aunts and uncles. *Le Monde*'s coverage differed from other publications which either printed scathing articles critical of the Church and Antoinette Brun or whole-heartedly supported those implicated in the case.

There are differing opinions among historians about the role that the press played in the resolution of the Finaly Affair. Historian Catherine Poujol argues that "The Finaly Affair was above all else a press campaign." If the media had been less involved and had not contributed to the polarization of the case, Poujol feels that the situation might have been resolved through the courts.[39] Katy Hazan, in her review of Poujol's, *Les Enfants Cachés,* disagreed with this conclusion. In Hazan's view, "the Finaly case cannot be reduced to a press campaign, which would suggest that it was fabricated or exaggerated." Hazan claims that the added religious dimension of a late baptism and the connivances of Antoinette Brun, who refused to comply with the court decision, set the Finaly case apart from others.[40] While I agree with Hazan, I also maintain the belief that the lengths to which Brun and members of the Catholic clergy went to prevent the return of two young "Christians" to their Jewish family was not only fodder for a media frenzy, but signified the continuation of Catholic antisemitism. Regardless of whether the coverage delayed or facilitated the boys' return to their family, a close examination of the coverage in *Le Monde* can lend important insight into the role antisemitism played for its decisionmakers, and thus advance our understanding of how antisemitism was perpetuated

after the war, even by those who had actively opposed the genocide of the Jews by the Nazis

and their helpers.

Post-war silence and the Holocaust

In this thesis, I argue that the press coverage of the Finaly Affair, which often promoted

voices that the Jewish community opposed, facilitated an early form of Holocaust memory in

the responses that were elicited from the Jewish side. Holocaust memory helps to ensure that

the history and lessons of the Holocaust help future generations understand the past and

develop a sense of responsibility for promoting a democratic, pluralistic future.[41] An area of

debate amongst historians is the topic of the silence of French Jews on Jewish matters, specific

to Nazi atrocities and the genocide of Jews in the post-war period. Despite the arguments of

some historians who contend that there was a "strange silence" from Jews, during the years

1952 and 1953, Jewish matters were actually in the spotlight. In addition to the Finaly Affair,

high profile cases such as the Slansky trial, the Doctor's Plot and the trial of Ethel and Julius

Rosenberg were in the headlines.[42] The press coverage of the Finaly Affair laid bare Jewish

matters, the memory of the Holocaust, and shaped the perpetuation of antisemitism after the

war.

As it will be illustrated in examples from the press, Jews did not refrain from discussing

the events of the Holocaust or referring to the over six million Jews who were killed when

discussing the Finaly Affair. Priscilla Dale Jones' research led her to argue that the Holocaust

was not mentioned in the coverage of the Finaly Affair.[43] In contrast, Daniella Doron contends

that despite the "strange silence" often referred to with regard to Jewish matters, a "lively debate ensued" in the French government and the public sphere on issues relating to Jewish youth.[44] The coverage of the Finaly Affair supports Daniella Doron's observation. The Holocaust was evoked in the pages of *Le Monde,* in more contemporary terms, by Jews and non-Jews multiple times. Although, as I argue, the Jews were put in a defensive position by the press, those who spoke out contributed to Holocaust memory. These early voices are important reminders to never forget.

To understand how the Jewish community and *Le Monde* were actually not silent on the topic of the Holocaust, it is essential to understand that the term "Holocaust," with a capital "H," describing the systematic mass killings of Jews by the Nazis between 1941 and 1945, only began to be used in the 1950s, and primarily by Jewish historians. Prior to this time there were some references to Nazi atrocities using "holocaust" in the sense of a "complete destruction of something; a mass slaughter, a massacre." More popular usages of the term "Holocaust," meaning the Nazi genocide of more than six million Jews, date from 1955.[45] *Le Monde*'s coverage of the Finaly Affair spans from the end of 1952 through the summer of 1953, predating the popular usage of the term. By focusing on other terms in *Le Monde*'s coverage that refer to what we today know as the Holocaust, we can see how both the newspaper and the Jewish community were not silent on the topic.

On February 20, 1953, *Le Monde* published "A Telegram to Pius XII from the Universal Israelite Alliance," an article that included a message that the Jewish organization had sent to Pope Pius XII, imploring "His Holiness" to intervene in the return of the Finaly children to their Jewish relatives. This was not the first instance that *Le Monde* published an article so directly supportive to a Jewish organization. Rabbi Jacob Kaplan, Chief Rabbi of Paris and leader of the

Central Consistory, which represented the Jews of France, published a "Mise au Point" on February 12 with the objective of setting the record straight on rumors already swirling about the Finaly Affair. It is notable that in February, *Le Monde* allowed slightly more coverage of the opposition. Prior to the statement from the Universal Israelite Alliance, three articles appeared with the opposing viewpoint. Despite the imbalance, the Alliance took advantage of this platform by leveraging their private message in *Le Monde.* By doing this, the Alliance was able to exert pressure on the pontiff to act, publicly declaring that the actions of the Church had not been effective in resolving the crisis. Over time, as this type of public pressure grew, it would push the pope and the Church to take more definitive action in the children's return. The tone of the organization's message is most significant not for its acquiescence, but rather for open reference to the Holocaust, suggesting that the refusal to return the children was rubbing salt in the wound of an already devastated Jewish community:

> The Universal Israelite Alliance, profoundly attached to the respect for the human person, expresses to the sovereign pontiff the emotion of the Jewish communities of the whole world, provoked by the non-restitution of the Finaly children, sons of Jews loyal to their religion, torn apart by Hitler in their French refuge and killed, to their anxious and close family members.

The message concluded by requesting "a personal intervention of your Holiness [Pope Pius XII] before the congregation of Notre Dame de Sion and others, which would permit a prompt conclusion to this painful affair and bring back a spirit of peace." At the end of their statement, they thanked the pontiff in advance with respectful gratitude.[46] The tenor of the message is urgent but remains cordial. There was still hope that the pope could intervene. This did not prevent the group from reminding the pope of how Hitler tore the Finaly family apart in their French refuge. At the publication of the Alliance's message, it had been 17 days since Robert and Gérald had mysteriously disappeared from their dormitory. As the weeks progressed, the anger and frustration of the Jewish community became even more palpable in *Le Monde*'s coverage. The cordial tone began to be replaced by anger as well as hopelessness. By June 1953, many Jews, including Moshe Keller, who represented the Finaly family, had lost hope that the Pope might intervene in the return of the children.[47]

In March, *Le Monde* added government voices to their coverage of the Finaly Affair. One member of the National Assembly, Monsieur Alix Berthet, representative of Isère, the region where the Finaly brothers were born, raised the issue of the Finaly Affair. He remarked on a particularly malicious campaign by politician Jean Ybarnégaray in response to the five priests who been arrested in the Basque region for kidnapping and abducting the Finaly brothers. These arrests occurred in February and the priests remained in jail contrary to the opinion of the Basque public who argued for their provisional release. Ybarnégaray, on his part, disseminated a pamphlet in the region supporting the release of the priests, which was enshrouded in antisemitism and called for violent protest.[48] In the 1930s, as a right-wing deputy for the Basses-Pyrénées region, Ybarnégaray is remembered for his response to the refugees who entered France following the Spanish civil war in 1939, many of whom were Jewish.[49] Ybarnégaray and members of his party, the Parti Social Français (PSF), resolved the crisis by housing the refugees in local concentration camps.[50] This type of solution foreshadowed the treatment of French and foreign Jews during the war, which also involved French camps. During the occupation, Ybarnégaray served in the collaborationist Vichy government and supported stricter anti-Jewish policies. With regard to Ybarnégaray's recent appeal, Berthet stated, "It is intolerable that we are threatened with an explosion of discontent if the incarcerated clergymen are not released, and that Monsieur Ybarnégaray, former minister of Petain, who remained silent when the Gestapo deported the resistant priests, is trying to stir up the Basque country." [51] In keeping with the relatively seamless re-integration of former Vichy collaborators in post-war France, Ybarnégaray re-entered public life and, was able to continue to spread antisemitic ideas throughout the community.[52] In this example, the violent appeal of a former Vichy minister triggered a member of parliament to speak out, evoking the memories of the Holocaust at the same time.

Le Monde's coverage of government affairs was not restricted to the French parliament. On June 25, 1953, just one day before Robert and Gérald Finaly would cross the border on their return to France, there was a meeting of the Israeli parliament. Benjamin Mintz, a deputy in the Israeli parliament demanded a general debate on the case of the Finaly orphans as well as all of the Jewish children not yet "incorporated into the Jewish nation." Mintz stated that "the Finaly Affair is the tragic symbol of millions of young Jews who still live in non-Jewish European institutions after the tragedy that befell Europe."[53] While using more vague terminology, it is implied that the "tragedy that befell Europe" refers to Nazi atrocities and the systematic genocide which occurred against the Jews during the Holocaust. Mintz's statement is also a reminder of the anxiety felt in the Jewish community about Jewish orphans who were still in non-Jewish custody after the war. There are a number of reasons why the Israeli government would raise the issue of the Finaly brothers as well as the broader issue of Jewish children who remained in non-Jewish custody. First and foremost, there was an intense interest in preserving Jewish culture in the wake of the Holocaust. Children were a sign of hope for the future of Judaism as well as Israel. Non-Jewish custody of children threatened to contribute to the erasure of Jewish culture. As a new state, founded in 1948, Israel also had an interest in augmenting its population. Many Jewish organizations, especially those who espoused more Zionist beliefs, helped to settle Jewish orphans in Israel. Additionally, it was well known by this time, that Robert and Gérald Finaly were destined to build their lives in the new state of Israel.

Secular organizations also leveraged the memory of the Holocaust and the persecutions suffered by the Finaly family to argue for the return of the children. On March 11, a press conference was held by the National Committee for Secular Action or CNAL (Comité national d'action laïque). This organization includes representatives from numerous French secular organizations including the Federation of National Education, the National Teachers Union and the Federation of Parent's Counsels for Public Schools among others.[54] Monsieur Albert Bayet made a statement as both the president of the League of Education and the President of the National Press Federation. There was no doubt in his mind that Dr. and Madame Finaly "clearly expressed their desire [for their children's future] before their deportation and deaths, that the children must be returned to their family."[55] While Bayet did not explicitly say how the Finaly parents expressed their desire, he was alluding to the fact that the children had been circumcised, in accordance with the Jewish tradition. This action, taken by the Finaly parents during the occupation, would be invoked multiple times by proponents of the Finaly family as justification for invalidating the children's Catholic baptism. These arguments will be expounded upon later in this thesis.

We also find that Jewish leaders recalled the atrocities of the Holocaust to support their arguments about the case. In the following examples, these leaders faced antisemitism in their appeals and responded by defending themselves and their community. In 1953, Rabbi André Zaoui, the leader of the Spiritual Movement for Liberal Judaism in France, attempted to meet with Monsignor Giovanni Montini, who was then the Pro-Secretary for Ordinary Affairs of the

Vatican Secretariat of State. History might have been different if the rabbi had actually been

able to meet with Montini, as he later became Pope Paul VI and was responsible for the

continuation of the Catholic Church's Vatican II reforms in the mid-to-late 1960s. But on March

12, Rabbi Zaoui met with Monsignor Dell'Acqua instead, the man entrusted by Pope Pius XII as

the Secretary of State's expert on all Jewish questions. Per archival records made accessible in

2020, we now know that Monsignor Dell'Acqua harbored antisemitic sentiments. Dell'Acqua let

his suspicions of Jews color his advice to the Pope. Concerning the proposed agreement to

return the Finaly children, Dell'Acqua stated that the result would most likely end "in favor of

the Judaic thesis." The children would end up "in the hands of Jews who, with ever greater

ruthless obstinacy, will force a 'Jewish' education on them, with the resulting humiliation of the

Catholic Church."[56] This finding, among others, illustrates that the Vatican was entrenched in an

antisemitic mindset during the war and post-war period, which influenced decision making.

Le Monde published Rabbi Zaoui's personal account of the meeting on March 17.

Zaoui's objective for this meeting was to ask for a solution to the Finaly Affair. He indicated to

Dell'Acqua that because the children were circumcised prior to being baptized in 1948, they

should remain Jewish out of respect for their parent's desires. He stated,

> The synagogue has a right to take back the children and raise them in the faith of Israel ... Because of the
> exceptional circumstances, the Church by a true measure of charity should go beyond canon law, should
> return the children to their religion of origin, it should annul the baptism and adopt a certain
> jurisprudence: love and justice must exceed the rigor of law.

This rather direct request must have rung in the ears of Dell'Acqua. He responded to the Rabbi

that the baptism was valid, and the Church could not abandon Catholic children. The children

should be free to practice the religion in which they were raised. Dell'Acqua then expressed to

Rabbi Zaoui that the issue would soon be resolved "because the children would return to France soon and should then be exempt from any pressure from the Israelites." To this the rabbi responded that "the young Finalys undoubtedly underwent pressure from Catholics, as their successive movements could only have been made under moral constraint and religious pressure." Zaoui cited the desire of the community to provide the children with instruction in Judaism and then give them the freedom to choose their religion at a later time. After paying homage to the Catholics who saved numerous Jews from death, Zaoui maintained "that the Finaly children should be returned into safe keeping" and described their baptisms as a "moral abuse." He, too, strengthened the resolve of his demand by raising the specter of the Holocaust: "I would like to believe and hope again, he concluded, in the name of six million Jewish martyrs, for a gesture of universal fraternity, the Catholic church should not accept this forced conversion."[57]

By April, the children had been missing for a month. Rumors circulated about where they were being hidden. One report, which was reprinted in *Le Monde* from a Madrid newspaper indicated that the French police were searching for the children in Brazil.[58] On April 4, 1953, as the concern for Robert and Gérald grew, *Le Monde* published a letter from Rabbi Jais, of the French Central Consistory, responding to statements by Abbot André Deroo, a Catholic priest and writer, which were published in *Le Monde* in March. Rabbi Jais, as part of the Consistory, strove to voice the opinions of the Jewish community in France. In his response to Abbot Deroo, Jais evoked the Holocaust using contemporary terms. He asked, who were the Finaly children? "Born in Judaism, confirmed in Judaism [by circumcision] at the height of Hitlerian persecution, sons of departed martyrs of their faith," became "orphan pupils of God" because a "reserved" group of believers decided to save them "through the renewed miracle of resurrection."[59] The rabbi went on to criticize Abbot Deroo for believing that Jews "are no longer the true Israel," Rabbi Jais then referenced the Jewish experience of the Holocaust in stronger terms:

> Despite praying in the language of David, meditating daily on the word of God as it came out of Moses' mouth, teaching love for one's neighbor and virtue, enduring more than anyone the stakes, gas chambers, and crematoria … It's all in vain! We would be fallen, damned, for remaining too faithful to the commandments of a law declared eternal by God himself.[60]

In the pages of *Le Monde*, Rabbi Jais, on behalf of his community, was able to express his anger with Abbot Deroo, a representative of the Catholic Church, for perpetuating a uniquely Christian form of antisemitism.

Chief Rabbi Jacob Kaplan of the French Central Consistory also made his feelings known by reminding his audience of the atrocities recently undergone by Jews during the Holocaust. On June 6, *Le Monde* published a statement Rabbi Kaplan made after participating in lengthy negotiations with the Church, the Finaly Family, and the Comité des œuvres sociales de la résistance (COSOR) for the return of the children. COSOR or the Social Aid Committee for Resistance Organizations, was a French government organization that initially grouped together the aid committees, established during the occupation, to care for resistance members and their families. After the war, the French Ministry of Prisoners of War, Deportees and Refugees mandated that COSOR provide for families who had been deported from France, regardless of their nationality.[61] COSOR became involved in the negotiations for the return of the Finaly children based on their role assisting deportees and their families. When the deadline for the children's return was not met on June 5, 1953, Jacob Kaplan showed his frustration by making a statement, which reverberated in the press. In it he solemnly affirmed "that he will never accept this stranglehold on the orphans, in contrast to the desires of the parents who were killed by the Nazis, and he will not remain an impassive witness to this offense against the memory of the martyrs of Judaism." Kaplan declared it his "sacred duty" to continue his actions so that cases like the Finaly Affair will not be conceivable anymore.[62] Kaplan did not hesitate to invoke memories of the Holocaust to support his argument. Other portions of his statement will be explained later in this analysis.

Although it is easy to perceive the Catholic Church as a monolith, individual members of the clergy actually voiced differing opinions. Jesuit priest and member of the French Resistance, Father Michel Riquet, was a unique voice in the Finaly Affair debate. During the war, Riquet opposed the Vichy government and helped more than five hundred Allied pilots escape from France, which led to his arrest in January 1944 by the Germans. He was interned at the Mauthausen and Dachau concentration camps and was freed by Allied forces in May 1945. As a sign that he stood in unity with those who were imprisoned and died in the Holocaust, Father Riquet wore his striped camp uniform during his first sermon at Notre-Dame-de-Paris after his return.[63] While the experience of priests interned at Nazi camps differed from those of Jews, Father Riquet's experience as a deportee factors into his position on the Finaly Affair and the humanitarian organizations with which he associated himself.

Throughout his life, Father Riquet campaigned against racism, serving as the Vice President of the International League against Racism and Anti-Semitism from 1972 through 1981.[64] At the time of the Finaly Affair, Father Riquet represented the position of the National Union of Associations of Deportees, Victims and Families of the Missing (UNADIF), for which he served as the Vice President. In an article first published in *Le Figaro* and later reprinted in *Le*

Monde, Riquet relayed that the primary mission of the organization was first to reassure the

public about the physical and moral conditions of the Finaly children and also "ensure their

return and stay in France, of which their father wanted them to be citizens," under conditions

that allow them to "become freely the men they have to be." In conclusion, Riquet stated that

French people of diverse political or religious affiliations are "united by the memory of their

common deportation" and were in agreement and resolved to act. Father Riquet ends with the

"hope that the parties involved accept the good offices offered to them by those who, through

the experience of concentration camps, are both more sensitive to the plight of the little Finaly

children and eager to prevent it from being exploited to revive a time when the French did not

love each other."[65] Although there was debate about whether Dr. Fritz Finaly wished for his

sons to be French citizens, overall, Father Riquet's message is empathetic to Jews and

acknowledges the common experience of deportation as a uniting factor. His statement also

illustrates a fear held by religious on all sides that the Finaly Affair would widen the gap

between Jewish and Christian communities and unleash antisemitic sentiments from the not-

so-distant past.

While the word "Holocaust," was not literally employed in *Le Monde*'s coverage of the

Finaly Affair, other terminology referring to the mass deportation and murder of Europe's Jews

was often used to evoke its events. As my analysis shows, *Le Monde*'s publication of the

responses of Jewish, Catholic, and secular figures to the Finaly Affair represents some of the

earliest post-war evocations of the persecution and atrocities of the Holocaust in the service of

support for Jewish, Catholic, and governmental causes.

Le Monde was more informed than other publications about the Finaly Affair due to its team of active correspondents onsite in Lyon, Grenoble and Bayonne. These correspondents wrote most of the day-to-day articles about the case.[66] Rather than have big name journalists of their own, *Le Monde* published articles from external writers such as Abbot André Deroo, a Catholic writer and priest, or Paul Benichou, a Jewish intellectual of French Algerian origin. *Le Monde*'s editorial team also had a preference for reprinting articles that had been published in other newspapers.[67] These articles by external contributors and those that were reprinted from other journals served as the backbone of *Le Monde*'s editorial program, in contrast to other publications who claimed well-known in-house journalists. In the case of the Finaly Affair, these articles contained most of the editorial commentary and will be a focus of the coverage in this thesis.

For the day-to-day details on the case, *Le Monde* relied on their team of special correspondents who reported from strategic cities. These correspondents were in most cases unnamed. At times, one could perceive the bias of the writer from their statements or inferences about the case, or by the headlines. More often than not, the correspondents presented the facts. When there is the appearance of bias it shows in the general support for returning the children to their relatives. Anticlerical sentiments can also be perceived in this coverage. For example, one article by a special correspondent was published just two days after Robert and Gérald Finaly's disappearance from their school in Bayonne on February 3, 1953. In the article, the correspondent presents his own hypotheses with regard to the scenario: "We thought at first that they had run away. But for what reason would they do that precisely on the day when representatives of their family were coming to reclaim them? There remains the second hypothesis: this was a kidnapping." The writer supports this proposition by citing the potential interference of Catholic lay people and clergy. Mademoiselle Setoan, a Spanish professor from the Notre Dame de Sion school in Grenoble, had come to Bayonne on February 2, 1953, the night before the children went missing. Her brother, Abbot Setoan, was a priest at the Saint-Louis-de-Gonzague school, where Robert and Gérald were enrolled. *Le Monde* reported that Abbot Setoan did not provide any information to the police when questioned, claiming to have been at mass at the time of the children's disappearance.[68] The article's commentary hinted strongly at the siblings' collusion in the kidnapping. Here we start to see the beginning of a pattern in the coverage of the case by *Le Monde* that represents a wall of silence on the part of the implicated clergy and lay people.

Mother Antonine, the Mother Superior of Notre Dame de Sion in Grenoble, was also suspected of having played a role in the abduction of the Finaly boys. She made headlines in *Le Monde* on five separate occasions. The headlines themselves tell a story of *Le Monde*'s coverage and how the publication leaned into the public's fascination with the arrested clergy. They illustrate the presence of anticlericalism and suspicion of Catholic collusion on the part of the writers. A similar pattern plays out with the coverage of the arrested priests. I will focus on the coverage of Mother Antonine to illustrate this point. Below are the headlines relating to her arrest and subsequent interrogations:

> February 6: "The disappearance of the Finaly children: Mother Superior of Notre-Dame-de-Sion in Grenoble is arrested"[69]
> February 13: "The Finaly Case: The investigation has gathered details about Sister Antonine's schedule and the children's stay in Marseille"[70]

First and foremost, the headlines amplify that Mother Antonine, a Mother Superior and more exalted member of the clergy, has been arrested in connection with the disappearance of the children. These headlines embarrassed the Catholic Church as an institution, creating a pressure on the ecclesiastical hierarchy to intervene in the affair. The headlines also tell a story of the multiple interrogations of Mother Antonine, caused by her evasiveness. In her first interrogation, Mother Antonine denied that Robert and Gérald Finaly were registered at the Notre Dame de Sion school in Marseille under false names. The interrogation also exposed that Mother Antonine ordered her sister, Denise Bleuze, to drive the children from Grenoble to Bayonne.[74] A second article from February 13, 1953, describes how the magistrates tried to reconstruct Mother Antonine's schedule before the abduction. The facts, as revealed in *Le Monde*, point to Mother Antonine's complicity in initiating the abduction after learning that the director of the school had disclosed Robert and Gérald's location to the authorities. When directly questioned Mother Antonine denied fault and claimed that she was in Paris when she first learned about the abduction in a newspaper.[75] In a third interrogation, which was reported on at the end of February after the authorities had gathered more information from warrants and testimonies, Mother Antonine began to sing a new tune, recalling her part in driving the Finaly children in 1950 from Paris to Grenoble to entrust them to Notre Dame de Sion Les Ancelles. She also admitted that the boys had been living under false names: Marc and Louis Quadri. Additionally, Mother Antonine confessed that she had been aware of the Finaly Affair since December of 1952 and that Mademoiselle Brun had accompanied her on her voyage.[76]

These remarks contradicted her previous testimonies. The coverage continued to build

throughout the spring of 1953. One can imagine the dramatic experience of *Le Monde*'s

readership hanging on each word to learn about the latest arrests, interrogations and lies

brought forth by the accused. The coverage rather than being supportive of the Church,

illustrated the deception of Mother Antonine. One can also consider what the reactions of the

Catholic clergy and lay people, who observed the drama, would be as they saw the events

playing out in France's newspaper of record.

Le Monde's choice to reprint articles from other publications and showcase outside

contributors rather than have their own in-house journalists raises some questions. Was this

editorial decision made to make *Le Monde* appear more objective? What was the publication's

motivation for showcasing these borrowed articles for their readership? Were the articles

complete or were portions omitted? Articles written by François Mauriac, a reactionary Catholic

writer, and reprinted in *Le Monde* can shed some light on the newspaper's motives. For

example, one article originated from an open debate about the disappearance of the children,

which played out in *Le Figaro*. *Le Figaro* was and continues to be a French national daily

newspaper with a right leaning outlook. In the article, François Mauriac responded to the

contention of Maître Maurice Garçon, the lawyer for the Finaly family, that it was only possible

later in life, when reason had come, that one could personally make a choice about their faith.

Le Monde printed excerpts of Mauriac's response from *Le Figaro* on the same day, titled "Will

you take the children by force?" Mauriac's statements were extreme. He flipped the script by

accusing Garçon of being the kidnapper, turning the accusation of kidnapping held by proponents of the family on its head and implying that the Jewish relatives weren't going to allow the children to make a choice regarding their own faith either. He asked Garçon whether, when the children are found, if he would use force to "tear them away from the Church and from France in spite of themselves?" If the children wished to remain Catholic, would Garçon "do violence to them?" Mauriac questioned how the lawyer felt he had the right to denounce Mademoiselle Brun of kidnapping when in fact, he maintained that the kidnapping had not yet taken place. "It's you who prepare yourself to perpetrate this, under the protection of the law."[77] In this instance, Mauriac's casting of Garcon as a kidnapper rather than a concerned supporter of the family provides one of the starkest examples of the perpetuation of antisemitism disguised as Catholic morality.

In another letter reprinted in *Le Monde* on March 4, Mauriac discussed the "flood of letters" that he had received in response to his two articles on the case, which were published in *Le Figaro*. One was signed by "An Unknown Jewish Voice," who indicated that they would add two more names to the list of the dead, referring to the genocide of the Holocaust. To this, Mauriac takes the opportunity to elevate Mademoiselle Brun and others like her on a pedestal:

> "Let my unknown correspondent make an effort to control his passion and to compare these two new 'dead' to the millions of those whom Robert and Gérald did not share the fate of because there were women like the nuns of Notre-Dame-de-Sion or like Mademoiselle Brun ... it is not enough to say that they were not martyrs. Those who erred in their regard sinned only from an excess of tenderness.

Mauriac also indicated that the "devout faithful of all Christian denominations" would find refuge with the Catholic hierarchy and in monasteries "until the end of time."[78] The difference between François Mauriac's bloated rhetoric and antisemitic sentiment and the relatively reserved language surrounding the case usually featured in articles in *Le Monde* is evident. I argue that, rather than promoting Mauriac's ideas on the Finaly Affair, excerpts of his letters were reprinted to represent the newspaper's distance from his antisemitism and to cast him as an outlier. The choice to reprint the articles also allowed *Le Monde's* readership to respond critically. For example, on March 2, Paul Benichou pushed back on Mauriac's accusation that Maître Garçon was in fact the kidnapper, stating that "Monsieur Mauriac is more serious when he calls the kidnapping an escape" as if the Finaly children were on vacation. He notes that Mauriac wrongly makes the accusation that the family are the "true kidnappers." Benichou "very much hopes that this devious conjuring has bothered his [Mauriac's] readers a little. It is too reminiscent of the judicial dialectics of totalitarian countries." [79] Benichou hoped that Mauriac's effort to spin the story would make his readers think twice and reflect on the rhetoric of totalitarian governments, possibly referring to the fascism and national socialism of the recent past.

It is clear that both Jewish and non-Jewish contributors to *Le Monde* were not silent about the events of the Holocaust when supporting their position on the Finaly Affair. *Le Monde's* use of special correspondents who reported from key cities closer to the events allowed for quicker reportage. By highlighting articles from other publications, *Le Monde* provided its readership with what was being said about the Finaly Affair in other publications of the time. The newspaper's editorial decisions to reprint specific articles or their extracts reflect subtle bias to the left of the political spectrum. A back-and-forth debate often ensued, allowing *Le Monde's* contributors to articulate their responses to issues. Their coverage and decision regarding the headlines of articles relating to the Finaly Affair also reflect a tendency towards anticlericalism.

Guardianship and Historic Catholic Antisemitism

Background on Catholic Antisemitism

In order to understand how new forms of antisemitism surface in the guardianship of the

Finaly Affair, it is important to understand the historical antisemitism that has played a role in

Catholic thinking and decision-making for two millennia. Christian supersessionism, or the belief

in the replacement of Judaism by Christianity, has formed the foundation of a particularly

pernicious form of antisemitism. As explained by historian James Carroll, Christian

supersessionism is the idea that the "Jesus movement," in its evolution into the Church,

replaced the Jews as God's chosen people.[80] For example, this surfaces in the nomenclature

used in naming the bible. The use of "Old Testament" rather than "Hebrew Bible "implies that

Christianity and it's "New Testament" sets itself above Judaism. This belief also played a major

role in justifying the conversion of Jews.

Proselytism is another facet of historical antisemitism that continued after the war. One

remarkable example comes from an essay by Rabbi Jacob Kaplan, called "Response to

Evangelists." It is dated September 23, 1947 and describes a pilgrimage to the Drancy

internment camp on the evening of Yom Kippur. Kaplan notes that a large crowd had come to

pray for the memory of their dear departed in the same place where they spent their last days

in France prior to deportation. Kaplan described the atmosphere as one in which the Jews

stood on "sacred soil, sanctified by the grandeur of sacrifice." The ceremony was to be

dedicated to memory and prayer, but once it began, Kaplan heard cries of indignation.

Someone had dared to distribute to this group "of grieving fathers, mothers, and children, to

these families mourning their dead, brochures in which they were invited to renounce the faith of our dear martyrs and convert to another religion." Remarking on the audacity of the

evangelists, Kaplan observed how "shamelessly" they "exploited the unspeakable suffering of

Israel, and the moral distress into which the Nazi persecutions plunged a certain number of our

brothers and sisters."[81] This is not the only example of overt Christian proselytism in France.

There was a "Christian Synagogue" run by Protestants in the 18th arrondissement of Paris called

"Beth El," created for the purpose of evangelizing Jews. Additionally, there was the "Eglise Juive

de Montmartre" or "Jewish Church of Montmartre," which was Catholic.[82] The order of Notre

Dame de Sion, who was complicit in the Finaly scandal, was also formed with the mission of

converting Jews to the Catholic faith. These are just a few examples of proselytism linked to

new forms of antisemitism that are relevant to post-war France.

The Jewish community was justifiably anxious about the kidnapping, proselytization, and

forced baptisms of their children, given that there had been earlier examples of kidnappings

linked to proselytism in Europe. Many have compared the Finaly Affair to the nineteenth

century case of Edgardo Mortara, which involved a conversion followed by a Church ordered

abduction. In 1855, when Edgardo was three years old, he fell gravely ill, and a household

servant took it upon herself to "save" him through baptism. Three years later, when he turned

six, the Church, after they learned of his baptism, took Edgardo from his home in Bologna, a

papal state. Edgardo would remain in Catholic custody and came to prefer it, completing his

Catholic education and becoming a priest. As a priest, Mortara often preached a narrative of

religious redemption and spoke out against his former community.[83] The Mortara Affair is

relevant to the Finaly Affair, first and foremost, because the Finaly Affair also involved a

baptism, which was administered without the permission of the parents, followed by an abduction, which the Church justified with canon law. The doctrine of canon law necessitated the separation of baptized Jewish children from all Jewish influence. Edgardo Mortara's acceptance of his conversion and subsequent transformation into a Catholic priest with an inclination to evangelize, was an example of both Jewish erasure and its perpetration. In the immediate post-war era, a time when the continuation of Jewish culture reached a new level of significance for Jews, the memory of this case was a threatening reminder.

Another aspect of Catholic doctrine that contributed to Jews' anxiety was that in 1953, the Catholic Church emphasized only one true path to salvation. This view promoted the belief that the Jews were widely understood to have not only rejected Christ as the messiah, but also were blamed for his death. Both of these aspects of church doctrine contributed to the perpetuation of antisemitism after the war. Even in the shadow of the Holocaust, these ideas permeated French society. It was not until 1965 and the declaration of *Nostra Aetate* by Pope Paul VI that the Church considered the validity of other religions, specifically mentioning Hinduism, Buddhism, Islam and Judaism. *Nostra Aetate* acknowledged that the Church had received the Old Testament from the Jews, who were described as people "whom God in His inexpressible mercy concluded the Ancient Covenant." It also recognized the "spiritual patrimony common to Christians and Jews" and recommended the fostering of mutual understanding and respect as well as a fraternal dialogue. Most significantly, *Nostra Aetate* retracts the charge that it was the Jews who killed Jesus, which historically fueled antisemitism and Jewish persecution, and stated that "the Jews should not be presented as rejected or accursed by God." The declaration specifically decried "hatred, persecutions, displays of antisemitism, directed against Jews at any time by anyone."[84] *Nostra Aetate* was the start of the Vatican II reforms, which among other updates, focused on interfaith dialogue. The Finaly

Affair was influential in bringing about *Nostra Aetate* and the reforms of Vatican II. It will be

illustrated in this thesis that more moderate voices did exist in the debate who advocated for

the Church to reevaluate its doctrine on baptism so that abductions, like those in the Mortara

and Finaly Affairs, would never happen again. With the reforms of Vatican II also came a

separation of Catholic missionary work from the Church's relationship with the Jewish

community. Judaism was officially respected as a true religion in itself and not a superseded

faith warranting proselytism.[85]

Coverage of the Finaly affair and its relationship to Catholic doctrine was also influenced

by the emergence of heroic narratives in many European countries that served as a

counterbalance to painful debates about Nazi collaboration. [86] These narratives, which served

as a way to save face nationally, found particular resonance in France, where the

collaborationist Pétain government became responsible for a large portion of persecutions

against the Jews via the creation of rigid laws that reinforced antisemitism. Catholics like

Antoinette Brun, who rescued Jewish children from Nazi persecution, became useful subjects of

these heroic narratives aimed at neutralizing painful memories of national collaboration.

Relevant to the Finaly Affair, Brun's generosity and her wholehearted devotion to saving

children were often acknowledged in the press. In an interview with *Match,* conducted after

Brun had been in detention for forty-two-days for failing to present the children in court, Brun

herself mentioned how she had saved nine Jewish children and adopted five. The popular

French view of Brun's activities was that she should be thanked for her humanity, saving

threatened children and violating the laws of the Vichy government.[87]

The actions of Antoinette Brun, to whom the children were initially entrusted, reflect how post-war church doctrine influenced the reception of the Finaly Affair in the press. The events were set in motion when Fritz and Anni Finaly left the children with their Catholic friend Marie Poupaert, who then attempted to confer the children to the Notre Dame de Sion convent in Grenoble. Since they were so young, nearly two and three years old, it was recommended that they go with Mademoiselle Brun at the municipal nursery. Robert and Gérald begun their time in Brun's custody in February of 1944. After the war ended, Margaret Fischl, Fritz Finaly's sister in New Zealand, wrote to the mayor of La Tronche, the town where the boys were located in Grenoble, to inquire about the fate of the family. On March 12, 1945, in response to her letter, the mayor informed her that sadly, her brother and sister-in-law had been deported to Drancy on February 14, 1944, but that Robert and Gérald had been saved and that they could be found at the nursery in Grenoble. He also told her that a friend of Fritz Finaly, Monsieur Ettinger, had been keeping an eye on the children. The mayor did not mention the name Antoinette Brun but did provide Fischl with Ettinger's address in La Tronche.[88] There was a relatively short span of time, one-year, from when the children were entrusted to Brun to when the family received news of the children's survival and began reclamation efforts.

Initially, when they first faced Brun's refusal to return the children to them, the family attempted to resolve the situation without litigation. In addition to contacting the Mayor as well as the Red Cross, Fischl also attempted to gain support from the Roman Catholic Church in New Zealand in order to resolve the issue. She reached out in 1948 to the Bishop of Auckland, who relayed Fischl's request to the Archbishop of Westminster in the United Kingdom. The

Archbishop then reached out to Monsignor Alexandre Caillot, the Bishop of Grenoble. In July

1948, Caillot responded to the Archbishop and indicated that he had had a long meeting with

Antoinette Brun and that the meeting ended with a very clear opposition on her part to the

request of the children's aunt. Unbeknownst to the family, Robert and Gérald Finaly had

already been baptized by this point in time.[89] It is possible that this was an unstated reason why

Fischl's outreach efforts to the Church did not yield a productive result. Around this same time,

Hedwig Rosner, the children's aunt in Israel, engaged Moshe Keller as the family's

representative in Grenoble. Keller decided to reach out to Mademoiselle Brun directly. Brun

refused to return the children and declared to him that she had the children baptized Catholic.

This was the first time the family was made aware of the baptism. After exhausting all non-legal

routes to the children's restitution and with the added variable of an illicit baptism, the

legislative battle began on January 7, 1949.

There would be four rounds of family court proceedings in the Finaly Affair. In early

June, 1950, the civil court of Grenoble declared the official deaths of Dr. Fritz and Anni Finaly to

have been on March 7, 1944. In France, children whose parents were deported were officially

under the provisional guardianship of the Departmental Offices of Veterans Affairs. Because

their parents' deaths were officially declared, Robert and Gérald Finaly would benefit from

provisions awarded to war orphans under an ordinance from April 25, 1945.[90] This change also

decreased Antoinette Brun's custody claim. On May 31, 1952, Robert and Gérald appeared at a

tribunal session. They declared that they wanted to stay with "maman Brun," but also affirmed

that they only saw her two or three times a year. Brun had attempted to repeal the outcome of

the fourth family council, however; on June 11, 1952, the court of appeals determined that the outcome of the fourth family court proceeding was valid and that Rosner would be designated legal guardianship. Brun was ordered to present the children.[91] When Moshe Keller and the bailiff when to Brun's home to collect the children on July 15, they had all disappeared.[92] Rather than return the children to their family, Antoinette Brun and members of the clergy circumvented French law and secretly moved Robert and Gérald between Catholic Church institutions, often under false names.

As outlined previously, Maître Garçon, himself a Catholic, questioned the motivations of Antoinette Brun in his statement to the Court of Appeals in Grenoble on January 9, 1953, which was printed in *Le Monde* the next day. He questioned whether Brun had a disappointed maternal sentiment or a type of imbalance. "If she took care of the children as a mother cat takes care of her kittens, we could say this." Garçon disclosed to the courtroom that "the boys had not been with her for several years." Regarding her evasion of the law, Garçon declared that it was "religious passion that pushes her to defy human laws … it is a crime in her view to dare influence the conscience of the children who had been baptized." Pointing out the hypocrisy of the situation, he reminded those present that "the Church is always opposed to these violations of conscience." Brun as a devout Catholic who benefited from the support of the Church, felt justified in baptizing Robert and Gérald Finaly. While generally, the Church was opposed to "violations of conscious," especially when it was a violation directed towards Catholics, like Protestant proselytism of Catholics for example, the Church appeared to have a double standard when it came to forced conversions of Jewish children.

It is important to know that Mademoiselle Brun, in addition to Robert and Gérald, claimed to have saved seven other Jewish children from Nazi persecution. This claim would become part of her story or rather, her heroic narrative. Brun would make this claim herself and likewise her supporters would accept and propagate it. There is evidence which casts doubt on this story in a testimony from Charles Kaufmann, Robert Finaly's "Gevatter" or godfather, to a judge in Vignon on June 4, 1953. Kaufmann claimed that after the Liberation he searched for the Finaly brothers. He went to the Château de Vif where he saw Robert, who recognized him, playing with another boy. The other boy was Guy Brun, a non-Jewish child whose mother abandoned him during the war. Brun legally adopted Guy during the war. He also saw Gérald who was sleeping in the house. Kaufmann saw no other children, which led him to believe that the story of saving additional Jewish children was Brun's invention.[93]

To understand her motives, we must also know that Mademoiselle Brun was a staunch Catholic and espoused the historically antisemitic idea that the Christians had replaced the Jews as God's chosen people. Brun also believed in one true path to salvation: Catholic baptism and Jesus Christ. In 1948, when she baptized Robert and Gérald, with full knowledge that their biological family was seeking them, Brun imposed her beliefs and views on the lives of two little boys. By doing this, she also contributed to the erasure of Jewish culture by replacing Jewish children with Christian children. While she may have saved them from death, her motives to keep the children after 1945 were undergirded by her antisemitic rationale, imposing an irreversible spiritual "saving" through Catholic baptism. Brun's acts are best understood as part of a culture in which Catholic clergy, officials, and lay people relied heavily on doctrine that was fostered during the war. As historian Saul Friedländer, who was also hidden in France and forcibly converted to Catholicism, has written, this culture included, "the strictest Catholicism, to an almost Royalist, ferociously pro-Pétain, antisemitic France."[94]

During the early years of the custody battle, the Finaly family made more direct efforts to personally work with Antoinette Brun. When Fritz Finaly's sister-in-law Augusta traveled to Grenoble in October of 1946, she sought out Brun and asked that the boys be returned. Augusta presented herself as the children's aunt when she arrived at Brun's door and implored Brun to return them. After explaining to Brun that the children were the only male descendants of the family and disclosing that her own husband was assassinated by the Nazis, Augusta was met with hostile comments. According to Augusta, Brun kept repeating that "the Jews are not grateful" and said that she would never return the boys.[95]

Another instance of hostility made by Brun and the Church occurred in 1948, when Otto Schwarz, Anni Finaly's brother, traveled to Strasbourg from Austria in an effort to have the boys returned. Schwarz expected to see his nephews. Instead, he was met by Brun, a Franciscan clergy member and two other men who urged him to sign an act which declared Brun the boys' legal guardian.[96] This episode illustrates the unwillingness of Brun to return the children and shows her strong desire to have them remain Catholic and to become their legal guardian. The presence of the clergy at this meeting also shows how the Church supported Brun, suggesting that both did so without regard to the millions of Jews who had been exterminated in the Holocaust in general, nor the pain and suffering already experienced by the Finaly family's losses in particular. These more direct efforts to reclaim the children, which were initiated with good intentions by the family, were met with hostility and, in Otto Schwarz's case, now included pressure to sign over legal custody to Brun.

The family's attempts to enlist the aid of other Jewish organizations elicited troubling information about Brun. In 1945, the family reached out to the Union of Jews for Resistance and Mutual Aid (UJRE), an organization that was founded in 1943 from the unification of various Jewish resistance movements to Nazism. These movements stemmed from the MOI which was the Immigrant Labor Force.[97] The UJRE then wrote to the Oeuvre de secours aux enfants (OSE), a Jewish relief organization, who investigated and found that Antoinette Brun actually lived in "precarious physical conditions" and was too proud to ask for aid. The OSE advised that it would be a good idea to send the children clothing and parcels. After Augusta's visit to Brun, the OSE decided to do its own investigation in September 1946. They learned that Mademoiselle Brun was happy to take these children away from all Jewish contact and make them into "good and true Frenchmen." This statement, implied that "good and true Frenchmen" were in Brun's opinion, Catholic Frenchmen and she would strive to keep the young Finalys on this path. The OSE, as a Jewish organization, supported the children's return to Judaism and their Jewish family, therefore they endeavored to do everything in their power to return them to Madame Fischl. [98]

Antoinette Brun not only refused to return the children, but also expected the Fischl family to pay their expenses. In an undated letter to Margaret Fischl, Brun informs her that her nephews are living in a home that required payment. Brun was known to turn away children who could not pay fees from her nursery.[99] Brun's decision to turn some children away to an uncertain future while accepting those who promised her remuneration no doubt played into her decision to save the Finaly children, although she claimed that her only motivation was the affection she had for them.

Classic negative stereotypes about greedy, wealthy Jews no doubt colored Brun's attitudes toward the Finaly family and her expectations for remuneration. For example, she cast doubt on the intentions of the Finaly family friends who were holding the property of Dr. and Madame Finaly. In a letter to Margaret Fischl, she told Fischl that "you do not owe anything to all the people who write to you asking for packages or anything else. No one has ever given anything to your nephews since they have been with me." Brun suggested that someone from the family make a trip to recover all that belongs to the children. It is hard not to jump to the conclusion that perhaps Brun wanted a cut of the inheritance for her troubles. In a passive aggressive way, Brun states that she has raised the children at her own cost without the support of any organizations.[100] Brun expressed to Fischl that she was "disgusted to see these people, so-called family friends, who want to take them [the children] away from me to share in their assets. Brun then described herself as French and Catholic, someone who had adopted seven other children and raised them with her own money and labor. Meanwhile, Moshe Keller, the Finaly family's representative in Grenoble, was convinced that Brun had possession of some of Fritz and Anni Finaly's property. Keller had noted that Brun was wearing a new mink coat, jewelry and also possessed a Leica camera. Robert, later in life said that he personally recovered some of his parents' items from Guy Brun, Brun's adopted son, including a pair of earrings, a gold watch, a diamond bracelet and his father's medical bag. This is evidence that Antoinette Brun had received the Finaly family property.[101]

Rumors circulated that Robert and Gérald had come from a family of financiers and stood to gain a large inheritance. *Le Croix* on February 27, 1953 reported that Dr. Finaly had eighty million francs. The children were related to banker Horace Finaly who ran the Bank of Paris and Paribas from 1916 through 1937, but they were not attached to any of the financial interests of this side of the family and merely inherited the surname.[102] While it is not certain if the children's association with Horace Finaly impacted Brun's attitude toward the children, there are indications that it may have made some difference.

The previous examples illustrate how Brun's attempts to evade the law and her willingness to engage in extended and agonizing court proceedings were linked to her explicitly antisemitic and hostile attitudes toward the Finaly family members. She was also happy to separate the children from Jewish influence so that the children could remain Catholic. However, her depiction in the press reflected similar attitudes toward Jews among the general population and helped to perpetuate antisemitism.

Depictions of Brun in the Press

The wide range of representations of Brun in the press is indicative of the role gender played in buttressing the utility of media reports of the Finaly Affair. From the start, Antoinette Brun was either an imbalanced religious fanatic or a saint who acted heroically as a member of the resistance. In 1953, Nicolas Baudy, a writer for *Commentary*, a publication of the American Jewish Committee, made note of her representation in the press when he wrote "who were these children who became stakes in a strange struggle," which "pitted a sadly tried Jewish family against a woman some regard as a saint and others a lunatic ...?"[103]

Le Monde's coverage of Brun provides examples of the way in which the press used standard gender tropes to cast a negative light on her actions. From the start, Brun lied about the family's reclamation efforts, saying that she hadn't heard from them. This is just one of multiple untruths disseminated with regard to the wishes of Dr. Finaly for his children and the amount of time it took for the Finaly relatives to begin reclamation efforts. In fact, the family had been pursuing custody since the moment that they learned the children had survived.

"Maître Garçon, defense lawyer for the Finaly family, set the record straight in his statement before the Grenoble court of appeals on January 9, 1953. "Mademoiselle Brun is an enigma," he declared. "Certainly, she presents herself as good, pitiful and maternal. We must acknowledge this. But she lied and maintained herself with a rare effrontery for three out of four years when she claimed that she hadn't heard anything from the family of these children."[104] Maître François Roche, a lawyer for Antoinette Brun, felt that the solution was to dismiss the case entirely. The president of the bar observed that Maître Roche painted a less somber portrait of Brun, by recalling for the court Brun's activities in the resistance. The court would make its decision on January 29, 1953.[105]

The court ruled against Brun and she was immediately taken into custody. Alexis Danan, who had written an article in *Liberation* just one month earlier with the goal to dissuade surviving deportees from reclaiming their children, wrote an article for *Franc-tireur* upon the news of Brun's arrest. Up until this point, representations of Brun in the press had been more supportive, even heroic. Danan's article, however, was far from laudatory, and he used gendered descriptions to denigrate Brun. The title, "Mlle Brun or the shrew that must be tamed," anticipates an injurious article. Danan's misogynistic portrayal of Brun precludes any support he may have given to her as an adoptive parent.

Danan represents Brun as someone who initially inspired trust and could impress others with her heroic past. With regard to the courtroom scene, Danan described "exasperated" judges who had "elegantly trusted" Mademoiselle Brun. Initially "superhuman emotion" was attributed to her and she was trusted to return the children on the appointed date and understand the grief of the Finaly family. Danan wrote that when given the opportunity to rescue the children, Brun "promised herself she would return them like the others when the time came." Then he said, "the miracle of makeshift motherhood knotted her entrails, and now returning them becomes an atrocious tearing away." Here Danan represents Brun as untethered when it came to the potential to have custody of the children and even more destabilized by the prospect that they would be taken away. He projected a form of maternal weakness on Brun and also implied that she was not mentally sound.

Danan also constructed Brun as a person who was devious and deceptive. Brun, according to Danan, scoffed at the grief of the Finaly relatives and "refused the court, with the same hostile and malicious face she had shown to the parents of the Finaly family [aunts and uncles], who had come from the other side of the world to thank her." Danan inferred that the court of Grenoble had had enough of Brun's farce and sent a message by convicting her. In closing, Danan stated that what was thought to be "crucified tenderness" was only "a grimacing stubbornness of an old maid with a dry heart, who claims to deserve heaven on the cheap, a heaven tailored to her measure."[106] Danan made use of colorful and misogynistic language to bookend his comments about Brun's arrogance in the face of the court and the Finaly family. According to him, Brun had fooled the court for a time and was now showing her true colors, which were anything but heroic.

François Mauriac, the conservative Catholic writer mentioned earlier, also deployed gender tropes in his writings supportive of Brun. He published an article entitled "'Will you take the children by force?." We have already touched on how Mauriac accused Maître Garçon, the Finaly family lawyer, and by extension the Finaly relatives of conspiring to kidnap Robert and Gérald from both France and the Church in section two. Mauriac also came to the defense of

Mademoiselle Brun. He questioned how Garçon and supporters of the family could accuse Brun

of kidnapping. He also expressed that he would pity Garçon for having to plead this matter

against Brun, whom he referred to as a "'monster of charity." Garçon could not "touch a hair of

this holy woman without raising the indignation of all of the Catholics in France as well as the

Jews." He remarked that "many Jews remember that she risked her life for them in dark hours,

that she loved them, loved them too much." Mauriac continued, "Miss Brun is one of those

criminals before whom for nothing in the world I would want to stand as accuser and judge."[107]

Brun was represented by Mauriac as unassailable as well as holy.

Jean Ybarnégaray, the conservative Catholic and former Pétain minister, also used

gender to express his support of Antoinette Brun. On February 26, 1953, he distributed a

violent appeal in the Basque country in defense of the arrested priests in the Finaly Affair.

Specific to Brun and her guardianship, he asked, "will we accept that two children are to be torn

away from their love for an admirable woman to whom they owe their lives, who has lavished

them with her dedication and affection, only to be delivered against their will by France to a

family they do not know and to a state they detest?" Ybarnégaray went on to exclaim that the

Jews were ungrateful for the efforts of the religious who risked their lives to save them. He

continued his appeal, leveraging his depiction of Brun against his depiction of Jews and also

added statements in which he claimed that Israel controlled the French government, the

assemblies and the courts.[108] With regard to Brun, he found no fault with her guardianship,

calling her admirable, and leveraged the potential separation of this loving mother from the

Finaly children as a fearmongering weapon to amplify support for the imprisoned clergy and

incite a future violent confrontation.

It was common for the clergy to use the press to support Brun's actions in their efforts to promote Church doctrine, and they, too, relied on common tropes of motherhood to do so. At times, they even used articles to place her on a pedestal as an example of a dutiful Catholic. Abbot Andre Deroo showed his support in a letter published in *Le Monde* on March 10. He said, "where it concerns the Finaly children, their baptism was provided on the initiative of Mademoiselle Brun. The children were orphans, and Mademoiselle Brun was their legal guardian." Deroo declares that Mademoiselle Brun was thoughtful and took care to raise the children with a Christian education. In brief, "she obeyed her conscience, she only did her duty."[109] We know now that at the time Brun was only a provisional guardian, the result of a family court proceeding which she manipulated by neglecting to disclose the efforts of the Finaly family to reclaim their nephews.[110]

Secular organizations also discussed Antoinette Brun. On March 11, 1953, the League of Human Rights and the National Committee for Secular Action (CNAL), an organization that includes representatives from numerous French secular organizations, met to discuss the "truth of the facts and their impact on the Finaly Affair." Monsieur Sicard de Plauzoles, president of the League of Human Rights, opened the session and referred to Antoinette Brun as "a woman of faith and duty," but emphasized that "the rights of children, hence those of humanity, had been violated." Mr. Forestier, general secretary of the National Union of Teachers took the floor. He declared that the members of the union of teachers also "pay homage to Mademoiselle Brun, who was pushed by her feelings to be an adoptive mother and wants by all means to keep custody of the children." The union said that they couldn't blame her as she was "confused" and "supported by the Church as she proceeded to violate civil law."

Maître David-Lambert, co-defender with Maître Maurice Garçon for the Finaly family, spoke next and retraced the events of the case. David-Lambert demonstrated that the uncles and aunts of the children had been interested in the fate of the children since the resumption of international relations. The family had never ceased to demand that the children be returned to them. David-Lambert expressed outrage with regard to the behavior of certain magistrates from Grenoble, whom he felt were too inclined to support Brun's evasions.[111] This example illustrates that the opinions of many of the spokespeople at CNAL and the League of Human Rights had mixed feelings about Brun, which were gendered. She was given credit for traditional feminine attributes like faith, duty and maternal feelings. Some even provided confusion as a possible reason for her actions, implying that as a woman she was more childlike and less responsible for her actions, than perhaps a man in her position would be. It was generally agreed that the rights of the children were violated and that the law was broken. Maître David-Lambert, for his part, was there to share the facts of the case with the organization. Unlike members of CNAL and those of the Human Rights League, the lawyer saw Brun as duplicitous and responsible for her actions.

Esprit magazine, a magazine focusing on politics, ideas and culture, provided an opposite representation of Antoinette Brun when compared to what was illustrated in the previous example. *Esprit* published a special issue on the Finaly Affair and extracts were reprinted in *Le* Monde on April 10, 1953. One extract came from an article written by Henri Marrou, a French historian and Catholic with a Christian humanist viewpoint. Marrou gave Brun very little latitude with regard to her actions in the Finaly Affair. He wrote, "it is too easy, he says, to 'give way' today to Mademoiselle Brun and to treat her uniquely as an 'old fool.'" In other words, Brun wasn't a confused foolish woman, her actions were premeditated. Marrou wrote that Brun waited until 1948 to baptize the children, a date when she was more certain about the death of the parents. Mademoiselle Brun may have thought she had sidelined the collateral relatives and that "French law would confirm her powers" as guardian, and that like "a mother, she became responsible for the natural and supernatural goods of the children." What was the cost? Marrou shared his dismay with readers regarding Brun's deceptions, which included not presenting the children in court and colluding in their abduction. He said that it was "very cruel for a Catholic to have to acknowledge that those of his sisters in Christ who claimed to act for the Church have so easily forgotten that Satan is 'the father of lies.'" Marrou affirmed that the baptism was at the very least a "grave imprudence," and that the "refusal to present the children to justice, their sequestration, and their abduction" constituted a fault and a crime. He declared in closing that the behavior of Brun, Mother Antonine, and all other complicit in the affair signaled "a resurgence of the time of clandestinity."[112]

Antoinette Brun, was not timid when it came to drawing out the legal process. The following example illustrates that Brun was not confused about her intent to retain guardianship of Robert and Gérald Finaly. All of her actions were for the purpose of delaying or obstructing the Finaly relatives from gaining custody of the children. In addition to her constant appeal for provisional release, she tried to appeal the decision of the last family court proceeding in the Finaly case, which had ruled on December 5, 1950, in favor of Hedwig Rosner as the legal guardian of the children. The Court of Cassation rejected this appeal and accepted the decision of December 1950. *Le Monde* published portions of the court report, which illustrated how Maître Goutet, Brun's lawyer, developed his arguments supporting the appeal.

Goutet spoke for two hours, first recalling the dramatic circumstances in which Brun had taken the children into her safekeeping. He acknowledged her "regrettable error" when she had the children baptized. Goutet believed that what Brun feared most of all was seeing the children who had been raised "the French way," which he stated was "their father's formal will." Goutet tried to evoke the emotion of his audience by stating that the boys would be "suddenly torn from our soil to be taken to Israel to live with an aunt who doesn't speak their language, whom they don't know, and whom they don't want."[113] This statement is oddly similar to what Jean Ybarnégaray stated about France, the Finaly family and the children's predicted move to Israel. What can be sensed is an overall sentiment of suspicion of the family and the new state of Israel. Many also assumed that because Robert Finaly was naturalized as a French citizen, it was the intent of the Finaly parents for them to grow up on French soil. There was no "formal will" as Maître Goutet had stated. It was more likely that if he and his wife survived, they would have joined their relatives in Israel. Like Ybarnégaray, the lawyer seemed to be projecting Anti-Zionist sentiments on the children and their "unwanted" future in Israel. As Brun's defense lawyer, Maître Goutet's statements also reflect her views. Goutet's comment about raising the children "the French way" recalls Brun's desire, as previously noted, to bring the children up as "good and true Frenchmen." The remarks appeal to a perception of French nationalism in which true French people are raised in the Catholic faith. The general suspicion and doubt cast on the children's future in Israel are evidence of anti-Zionist sentiments, which also reflect on Brun. In summary, while she was portrayed as either faithful to her religion, a loving mother, confused or even imbalanced, these examples show that Brun's actions were purposeful and that she intentionally broke and obstructed the law.

As the Finaly Affair progressed, inaccurate information circulated about the wishes of

Dr. Fritz and Anni Finaly for the future of their children. Maître Goutet's claim that the Finaly

parents wished for their children to remain in France is just one example where the truth was

twisted to support a rationale that propped up conservative viewpoints. The Defense

committee for the Finaly Family released a statement on June 18, 1953. In it they wished to set

the record straight on Fritz Finaly's intentions for the boys' future. They acknowledged that

Robert Finaly had been naturalized in 1941 and that this had been "interpreted in articles and

interviews, recently published in the press, as a desire for them to stay in France." They

affirmed that "this was just an interpretation of a fact" and there were "other equally plausible

hypotheses undermining the value of this interpretation." The committee asserted that the

Finaly parents, as Austrian refugees, were considered to be enemy nationals. They naturalized

their son as a protection measure. The committee also argued that Dr. Finaly had been a

longtime Zionist and was a card-carrying member of Zionist organizations in Austria up until

their departure. Because of Dr. Finaly's faith in the future of Palestine, one could assume that

"if the Finaly parents had survived, they would have gone to Israel, where Dr. Finaly could have

practiced his profession, which he could not legally do in France." The committee charged that

interpretations of Fritz Finaly's intention to raise his children in France and the general

disregard of his formal desire to raise the children in Judaism, which was affirmed by

circumcision, were violations against the wishes of the parents.[114]

The evening of June 27, 1953, brought the long-awaited news of Robert and Gérald

Finaly's return to France. According to the press, several personal friends of Mademoiselle Brun came to support her at the municipal nursery. Brun "categorically refused to make a statement." Brun's friends however described her as being "devastated."[115] Rather than be enthusiastic about a chance to see the children again, it seemed she was more disappointed that they were now out of hiding. Perhaps she worried that the world would learn the truth about her guardianship, particularly her proximity to the children over the years. Despite what Brun and certain ecclesiastics wanted to represent, Robert and Gérald were not in her constant custody. In fact, the children spent most of their time moving from institution to institution. Maître David-Lambert, part of the Defense Committee for the Finaly Family stated, upon the children's return, that their experience had been detrimental to the children's education. "The education of these children has been particularly neglected," he said. "Gérald had boasted of having attended about fifteen different institutions." Specific to Brun, he noted the relatively short time period that the children could have been separated from their family had Brun given them back. Brun, "of her own volition, assumed the role of their mother and obstinately refused to return them to their family after less than a year of separation to entrust them to various religious institutions." David-Lambert described Robert and Gérald as enthusiastic and making plans for their stay in Israel. He also described Rosner as determined to raise them with absolute respect for the opinions and tastes of their parents, and above all, with respect for their own personality."[116]

The children would arrive in Tel-Aviv with their aunt on July 26, 1953. After transitioning in France for a month, Rosner and the children departed more suddenly than anticipated for Israel because they feared that there was a chance of a new abduction.[117] Mademoiselle Brun felt affronted by the departure. After nine years of an anguishing custody battle, she was not ready to give up. On July 30, together with her lawyer, Maître Floriot, Brun shared her intention to send the President of France, Vincent Auriol, a letter demanding that he do all in his power to obtain the return of the Finaly children. Brun also expressed her feeling about the departure of Robert and Gérald. She commented that the "brusque and secretive departure" of Robert and Gérald Finaly did not surprise her. She never believed in the sincerity of the agreements that were made and that no one consulted her about. Brun claimed that she only wanted one thing: "To see for a last time my little ones and tell them that wherever they are they will always be my little ones and that they will always have a place in my heart. This, Madame Rosner refused me." Brun claimed that Hedwig Rosner did everything in her power to prevent her from succeeding and alleged that Rosner was afraid "that if the children were brought into my presence, they would confirm their desire to stay in France with me." Brun went on to discuss her hardship throughout the legal proceedings and accused Rosner of refusing to appear in court, she also accused Rosner of secretly taking her [Brun's] children to Israel under false names and by force, to prevent her from her right as a French person to regain custody.[118]

By closely examining the guardianship of Robert and Gérald Finaly by Antoinette Brun, we can perceive her traditional Catholic antisemitic views. She felt entitled to baptize these children while violating the wishes of the Finaly parents who had circumcised their children with the intent to raise them in Judaism. Her defenders, who were largely conservative and Catholic described her as a "monster of charity" and a "holy woman." By initiating the baptism and providing a Catholic education to the children, they affirmed that Brun was doing her duty, while turning a blind eye to thoughts that Brun may have been otherwise motivated. Even the teacher's union described her as "confused." Often evoking her heroic and selfless past, it was too easy for Brun's supporters to condescend to chastising the Jews for being ungrateful. Augusta, Fritz Finaly's sister-in-law, was the direct recipient of such comments from Brun. Jean Ybarnégaray would repeat the sentiment in his appeal in support of the jailed priests in the Basque country.

There is an anti-Zionist element to the affair, which surfaced as suspicions about Israel and the family's intent to take the children there. Both Jean Ybarnégaray, a former Nazi collaborator, and Brun's defense lawyer, Maître Goutet, would have been happy to see the children stay in France with Mademoiselle Brun rather than live in Israel, which they both implied was undesirable. An OSE report also highlighted how Brun was keen to bring the boys up as little Frenchmen and keep them separate from Jewish influence.

Perhaps drawn in by the connection of the Finaly brothers to financier Horace Finaly or the information she learned about the property that the children were entitled to, Brun was unusually fixated on money. While she disparaged friends of the Finaly family for not bringing packages or implied that they coveted the Finaly possessions for themselves, Brun portrayed herself as a martyr who took in many children and raised them with her own money and desired only affection in return. One of those children, Guy Brun, many years later, restituted some of the Finaly possessions to Robert, evidence that Brun had possession of the Finaly property. [119]

Barring his misogynistic comments, perhaps Alexis Danan was correct in his characterization of Brun. She was persistent until the end, declaring that she would write to the President of France. By looking at this complicated guardianship case, we can see how antisemitic ideas and sentiments were perpetuated in numerous ways. We first see this in

Brun's traditional Catholic beliefs and her self-authorization to baptize the children. As we dig deeper we can observe Brun's total disregard of the Finaly family's wishes and the impact that the Holocaust had on them and their family structure. It is also notable that Brun may have had illusions of a possible inheritance. The press, an actor in itself, by bringing the events of the affair to a public forum, invited debate from all ranges of the political spectrum.

What is Special about Catholic Baptism?

Background

Baptism, on its surface is a "Christian sacrament marked by ritual use of water and admitting the recipient to the Christian community."[120] The timing and implications of baptism differ among Christian denominations. Here, the focus will be on the sacrament of Catholic baptism, which historically has been regarded by Catholics, as the one true path to spiritual salvation. This sacrament is inclusive of specific ideas, tied to canon law, which perpetuate historic antisemitism such as Catholic supersessionism, indifference to the faith and family of non-Catholics, and a preference to baptize children rather than adults. As this paper will illustrate, these uniquely Catholic preferences and ideas related to baptism played a role in the Finaly Affair. The baptism and subsequent abduction of Robert and Gérald Finaly, brought into the 20th century, Church doctrinal issues which first arose thirteen-hundred years prior.[121]

The sacrament of baptism is unique in that its success depends on the complementary Catholic education of the receiver.[122] It was preferred to convert children rather than adults who had already formed ideas about themselves and the culture that they identified with. Baptizing children presented a solution to the difficulties of converting adult non-Christians. It was expected that when baptized, one would select a Christian name as well as separate oneself from non-Catholic family members or cultures. As Elsa Marmursztejn explains, the

scenario is presented as a way to save children; however, the forced integration of children into

a dominant group reveals that a manipulation of memory is playing a role in these efforts. A

child's memory can be formed, and a Christian identity can be constructed with the

prerequisite destruction of their original way of living.[123] When a child is baptized, at a time

when they do not have agency to separate themselves from their Jewish origins, the Catholic

Church would step in to assure this separation. As in the Finaly Affair and several other high-

profile cases, the Church has been accused of abducting children for this reason.

This scenario of converting children played out in numerous artificial family structures,

which were created during World War II and would continue into the post-war period. Jeann

Duns Scot, a Franciscan, contended that the descendants of baptized Jews would be truly

faithful in three or four generations. He also argued that infants raised by faithful Catholics and

instructed in their law, would acquiesce to the law.[124] It is disturbing to consider that after

several generations Jewishness could potentially disappear. In some post-war cases, the

erasure happened much more quickly. Jeannine Glass had been entrusted to the Lagoutte

family during the war and grew up estranged from Jewish religion and culture. Although

archival evidence does not show whether the Lagoutte family had imposed Catholic baptism on

Jeannine or whether Jeannine decided to convert, she left the Lagoutte family convinced of her

Catholic faith and hostile to the idea of leaving her adoptive family.[125] The idea of hidden

children, and examples like those of Jeannine Glass, who remained in non-Jewish custody,

caused intense anxiety in the Jewish community. A World Jewish Congress memorandum

dating from March 7, 1945, seems to sum up the anxiety of the time. "The first phase of the tragedy of contemporary [Jewry], the physical destruction of millions of Jews, is nearing its end, and already the second phase is setting in, the phase of destruction through baptism.[126] There was perceivable concern, just after the war, that although the events of the Holocaust had ceased, a more subtle erasure was being inflicted on the Jewish community through conversion.

Catholic Church law, known as the Code of Canon Law, has been a gray area with regard to the baptism of non-Christians. By the 14th century, Catholic law had begun to narrow the options for those who converted to the Catholic faith. Forced conversions were forbidden in the law and continue to be forbidden today. Canon law dictates that for an infant to be baptized, one parent or guardian must consent. The same section of the law also states that infants can be licitly baptized against the parents' will if the child is in mortal danger. It also states that those who are already baptized whether licitly or illicitly should remain Catholic.[127] This doctrine has been held by the Catholic Church as a reason not to return converted Jewish children to their Jewish families of origin. It is believed by the Catholic Church that those who have already been baptized should remain Catholic or in the eyes of the Church commit the mortal sin of apostasy, meaning that a converted individual goes back to their former religion. Historian Jessie Sherwood contends that there is still disagreement about the precise rules or demands of canon law pertaining to baptism.[128] The uncertainty of how to apply the law continued into the post-war era. The press coverage of the Finaly Affair reveals disagreement between Catholic clergy and lay people on the execution of doctrine relating to the baptism of the Finaly children. This will be explored further in the next section.

A document authored by the Vatican in 1946 and unearthed in the 2000s caused new

controversy. This document made it evident that the Pope and Vatican officials espoused a rigid

view of canon law in the immediate post-war period. Written on October 23, 1946, The

document was discovered and published by historian Alberto Melloni in the Corriere Della Sera,

an Italian daily newspaper, in 2004. This publication caused a stir about Catholic intentions to

kidnap Jewish children. The *New York Times* referred to the document as "cold and impersonal"

and added that it made no mention of the Holocaust.[129] The Vatican document itself did not

specifically refer to kidnapping, but instead focused on Jewish children in Catholic custody. It

was sent from the Vatican's Congregation of the Holy Office in response to a letter from the

Paris Nunciature, headed by Monsignor Angelo Roncalli, asking Pope Pius XII for guidance on

the situation of Jewish children in Catholic custody.

In the 1960s, Roncalli, as Pope John XXIII, would be the force leading up to the Catholic

Church reforms of Vatican II. In 1946, however; such reforms and the thought of being more

inclusive toward non-Catholic faiths was not common. The determining factor in returning the

children was whether they had been baptized or not. Approved by Pope Pius XII, the document

included five stipulations about Jewish orphans in Catholic custody. The first condition was that

nothing be put in writing. Second, the Church would investigate each case separately. The third

provision was that children who were baptized could not be given to institutions who could not

assure their Christian education. If the children had not been baptized, the fourth stipulation

indicated that because the Church had taken care of them, it was not appropriate that they be

entrusted to "people who have no right to them" until at least the age that they could consent.

The final proviso was that if the children were entrusted to the Church by their parents, were not baptized, and their parents claimed them, they could be returned.[130]

The Holy Father approved the instructions, which were evasive and did not take into consideration the hardships that the Jewish community had gone through and continued to suffer in the aftermath of the Holocaust. If anything, they delayed the efforts of families to reunite with their young relations. The Church imposed extra hardship on the families whose relations had been baptized without the family's permission, as in the case of the Finaly brothers. The instruction that nothing should be put in writing eschews the possibility that there would be a written record of the decisions. The instructions also reinforce the traditional catholic antisemitic view that once a child is baptized into the Church, they need to be separated from all Jewish influence including their families.

Underscoring this Catholic belief, a letter from Pastor Daniel Atger of the Reformed Church of France, referenced an instruction from the Vatican's Congregation of the Holy Office, the authority on Church doctrine, which reminded Catholics of the need to separate converted Jewish children from all Jewish influence in 1777. "It stated that it is necessary to assure the Christian education of the baptized, which makes it necessary to separate them from their parents. The Church is also a mother; she has the right to keep watch over the religious education of her children and remove any obstacles that oppose it; She is unable to leave the baptized exposed to the imminent danger of apostasy."[131] The gendered representation of the Church itself is particularly interesting, as if "She" became the guardian, once baptism took place. The gendering of the Church as a mother to the faithful will be echoed by Catholic thinkers in the press in their responses to the Finaly Affair.

Ironically, an institution that many associate with a male hierarchical leadership, has been strategically described as the spiritual mother of the faithful. In fact, the Church and the Synagogue have been personified in art as female for thousands of years. There are numerous extant examples of this personification in religious iconography. In the typical portrayal of Ecclesia, representing the Church, and Synagoga, representing the Synagogue in art, Ecclesia faces Christ and receives his blood and is blessed. On the left side of Christ, Synagoga is blindfolded and physically turns away from Christ and salvation.[132] Synagoga's placement to the left of Christ in iconography is significant because the left signifies the sinister as compared to Ecclesia's exalted placement on Christ's right side. In this example Synagoga's staff is broken and her crown has fallen off. A monster appears from below, possibly hell, and threatens her. This imagery is an example of how Catholic Christians visually showed how Christianity both inherited and superseded the rich spiritual history of Judaism.

Figure 1 Christ choosing 'Ecclesia', chasing away 'Synagoga'[133]

Abbot Deroo referred to the Church as a mother in his argument against secularism: "When we talk about the problems that are raised due to the Finaly case, we practically prevent ourselves from reaching a reasonable and valid solution if we exclude essential factors, which are the rights of God, the supernatural destiny of souls, and consequently, the duties and rights of the Church," described as "the 'mother' of the faithful who is entrusted with the duties of teaching and sanctification." Deroo's sentiments showed Catholic exceptionalism in the way in which he placed the Catholic Church on a higher plane than other faiths, like Judaism. He believed that the souls of Jews and non-Catholics would not meet their "supernatural destiny."

The press, during the Finaly Affair, provided Catholic clergy and writers with a platform to air their thoughts and ideas on the case and its relationship to church doctrine. It is evident from the coverage that there was disagreement, as we will see, among Catholics on the doctrine of baptism and whether the Finaly baptisms were licit. This supports Jessie Sherwood's argument that there is still disagreement about the precise rules of canon law pertaining to baptism.[134] The coverage also reveals that support for Antoinette Brun's decision to baptize Robert and Gérald was a common theme among Catholics. This illustrates the persistence of a traditional belief among Catholics that Christianity has replaced Judaism and offers the true path to salvation. Also discernable from the media coverage of the case is a general Catholic disregard of the impact these actions had on Jewish culture and families, especially after the events of the Holocaust. Catholics featured in the press rarely addressed the fact that Antoinette Brun had her own motivations for initiating the baptisms of Robert and Gérald Finaly, beyond merely doing her Catholic duty.

However, there were some lone Catholic voices that explicitly opposed her decision. Father Michel Riquet, a former deportee himself, believed that the baptism of the Finaly children was invalid because their parents had had them circumcised. This was a belief shared by both the Jewish community and the Finaly family. While he adhered less to traditional Catholic thinking on this point, Riquet gave Antoinette Brun a pass for her behavior because she was obeying Catholic law. Riquet did recognize that Brun was legally wrong not to return the children when the court of Grenoble had ordered it, but he also stated that in the absence of the boy's parents she was their "spiritual matrix" and educator and had adopted an "understandable" attitude.[135] To Riquet, Brun was assuming the expected duty of a Catholic woman. Her behavior was also in step with traditional expectations of working with converts. Riquet did not acknowledge that Brun might have had some personal motivation to baptize the Finaly children at a time when the threats of war had long passed, and she knew that the boys' Jewish family was seeking custody.

Most of the Catholic Church representatives whose opinions were published in the newspaper supported Brun. Abbot André Deroo was a French writer and representative of the Catholic Church who often authored letters published in *Le Monde*. Allowing Deroo to leverage the press as a platform for his traditional Catholic beliefs, especially in the area of baptism, is one way that *Le Monde* allowed the perpetuation of ideas which were undergirded by historic Catholic antisemitism. Abbot Deroo supported Antoinette Brun's decision to baptize the Finaly children. A letter submitted to *Le Monde* and published on March 10, 1953, illustrates these points and evoked a large response. In his lengthy letter, which was broken down into sections, Deroo discussed the views of the Church, the familial bond, the rights of God and the supernatural destiny of souls, and the Church's duty. The motivation for his letter was *Le Monde*'s "Free Opinion" section, published on March 1, 1953, which featured the opinions of three diverse thinkers. In Deroo's words, *Le Monde* was "displaying, as is its custom, a broad eclecticism."[136]

Disagreements played out in letters to the editor, in which positions were asserted and opposed. These often either reinforced this new form of antisemitism, while others evoked the murder of six million Jews in the Holocaust in order to buttress support for the return of the children. The letters, which were published by *Le Monde* in March and April of 1953, indicate the varying angles in the debate on the Finaly children's baptism. The first letter came from

Paul Benichou, a Jewish French Algerian associated with intellectual movements. In his letter

Benichou accused the Church of having a double standard when it came to the definition of

family, which depended on whether the family was Catholic or non-Catholic.[137] Abbot Deroo's

letter from March 10 responded to Benichou's analysis of the Finaly case, specifically

Benichou's charge regarding the Church's view on family.[138] An additional letter, published on

April 10, by an anonymous Catholic will also be analyzed as it represents a moderate voice in

the debate on baptism.

On March 2, 1953, *Le Monde* published Paul Benichou's letter. In this letter, Benichou

accused the Church of seeing "the family as a family of law when it is Catholic," but that when it

is non-Catholic, the family is considered "more a grouping of facts, provisionary, illegitimate …

The Catholic family is sacred; the non-Catholic family is nothing: the sacrament of baptism,

when you touch it [the non-Catholic family], it is crushed."[139] Benichou's statement asserts that

it takes only a single blow through Catholic baptism in order to destroy a Jewish family. Readers

who were familiar with the Finaly Affair would have understood how the children's baptism

changed the battleground in the custody debate. If the children had not been baptized, the

Church would have been more apt to return them. Because they were baptized the family and

children would be separated for nine years.

In a rebuttal to Benichou, Deroo defended the Church, claiming that it "respects familial

rights, but cannot evade its own duties." He presented the act of baptism as an irreversible

procedure, claiming that "baptism confers upon the child a Christian character," after which the

infant is under the jurisdiction of the Church. The Church has the responsibility to ensure its members have the means and benefits of supernatural life, which surpasses the mere demands of the natural order in dignity and value." Deroo's comments not only project a diminished value on non-Catholics, but he also implies that divine law supersedes the "demands of the natural order in dignity and value," which according to Deroo justifies the Church's intervention in past cases involving both baptism and abduction such as the Mortara Affair.[140]

Revisiting the matter of the baptism of Jewish children in general, Deroo indicated that the "discipline of the Church is consistent and clearly defined." Deroo described Jews as "infidèles" or unfaithful and further wrote that when "examining the scenario of a baptism of an 'infidèle' who becomes Christian despite the wishes of their parents...one must keep the child, remove him from the hands of his parents, so that he may be raised in a pious and holy manner."[141] Deroo openly supported the idea that the Finaly brothers and other baptized Jewish children should be removed from their parents' custody, by whatever means necessary, so that they may be raised and educated as Catholics.

Unsurprisingly, Deroo is supportive of the role of Antoinette Brun in the children's baptism, and, unlike Father Riquet, does not raise the issue of how Brun had broken civil law. Instead, Deroo doubled down on his support by praising Brun's initiative in baptizing the orphaned children and insisted that Brun was their legal guardian. She "acted with thoughtfulness" and "took care to raise the children and gave them a Christian education. In this she obeyed her conscience. She only did her duty."[142] Perhaps unbeknowst to Deroo, Brun was actually only the provisional guardian at the time of the baptism in 1948.

Reflecting a more flexible point of view, an anonymous Catholic writer sent *Le Monde* a letter, which was published on March 10, 1953. This writer separated himself from the ecclesiastical hierarchy, like Deroo, who were able to take a position in the public debate, as a common Catholic. He remarked that the clergy who had spoken out adhered to doctrinal rules that had been imposed by the Catholic Church "since high antiquity." Where his view, and therefore that of the common Catholic's, diverges from clergy members in the debate is whether the baptism has sacramental value or not. The anonymous Catholic then suggested a more flexible way to look at the sacrament. He remarked, "It seems to us on this point the doctrine of the Church demonstrates a strange static nature when compared, for example, to the canonical rules concerning marriage, which are more flexible in practice." When the Church "dissolves the marital bond, it does not break anything; it merely acknowledges that this bond is in fact and in law nonexistent, and it draws the necessary conclusions." He noted that even when one or more children are produced in the marriage, the Church still allows the marriage to be annulled in certain cases. For example, it might be annulled if one spouse was coerced into the marriage. With regard to Catholic baptism, which is usually administered to children who are spoken for by others, he asked why shouldn't these also be considered for annulment?[143] While not conceding that the Church coerced the Finaly children in any way, this anonymous writer does recommend that the church reconsider its flexibility on the doctrine of baptism.

These examples from a variety of Catholics illustrate how historic antisemitic themes were used to support arguments about doctrine, even by leaders who surely did not support the genocide of the Jews. These themes include Catholic exceptionalism, with regard to families and faith, as well as the idea that there is one true path to salvation. The idea that after baptism, it is necessary to separate the converted child from Jewish influence and provide them with a Christian education surfaces often in the press coverage and is a clear example of the persistence of Catholic antisemitism. In fact, Antoinette Brun is lauded by both Father Michel Riquet and Abbot Deroo for educating Robert and Gérald Finaly, even though Riquet considered the baptism to be invalid. We also see the beginnings of a debate about the Church's strict adherence to doctrine and whether it continued to be productive or was outmoded. Newspapers like *Le Monde* provided a platform for these Catholic writers and, whether intentionally or not, allowed for the perpetuation of historically antisemitic ideas, particularly those of Abbot Deroo, which were printed and potentially co-opted by others. As we will see next, there was a significant response to Deroo's comments and the Finaly Affair from the Jewish Community.

The Jewish Community on the Defense

The Jewish community voiced its opinions through well-known individuals as well as organizations. Their contributions were primarily defensive measures against traditional Catholic antisemitism and rumors which began to circulate around the case. Several eminent rabbis and Jewish organizations were outspoken about the Finaly baptism and insisted that the boys had already been confirmed into Judaism by Dr. Fritz and Anni Finaly when the children were circumcised. In addition to offering early examples of Holocaust memory, Jewish writers and organizations also used the press as a platform to contribute to a wider understanding of Judaism. *Le Monde* published many contributions from the Jewish community, which grew increasingly emotional after February 1953, in parallel with the ever-increasing time that children remained missing.

Soon after the abduction of the children from their school in Bayonne, Rabbi Jacob

Kaplan, the Chief Rabbi of Paris, aimed to counteract numerous rumors that had already been

circulating in the press regarding the case. Kaplan's "Mise au Point," or clarification, was

published in *Le Monde* on February 12, 1953. Pertaining to the children's baptism, Kaplan

confronted the rumor that prior to their deportation the Finaly parents requested that their

children be converted to Catholicism and kept away from their relatives. Kaplan retorted that

"Doctor Finaly circumcised the children during the occupation, proof of his fidelity to Judaism …

and expressed the desire to see them raised by his sisters, in the case that he came to

disappear." Another rumor was that Fritz Finaly's sisters had waited years before getting news

on the children and attempting to reclaim them. Rabbi Kaplan confirmed that this was untrue,

and that the family had engaged in uninterrupted efforts to find the children since February

1945. Kaplan also opposed the rumor that Antoinette Brun had baptized the children at the

family's request. Kaplan provided evidence that the opposite was the case: Brun had lied to one

of the aunts when she wrote to her that "your nephews are Jews. In other words, they will stay

in their religion."[144]

Rabbi André Zaoui, leader of the spiritual movement for liberal Judaism in France, like

Kaplan, believed that because Robert and Gérald Finaly were circumcised upon the decision of

their parents, they should remain Jewish out of respect for the wishes of their parents. On

March 12, 1953, Rabbi Zaoui met with Monsignor Dell'Aqua at the Vatican to discuss the Finaly

case. Zaoui's recollection of the meeting was published in *Le Monde* five days later. Based on

the facts of the case, Zaoui told Dell'Aqua that the Synagogue had a "right to take back the

children and raise them in the faith of Israel." Zaoui also expressed to Dell'Aqua that due to the circumstances the Church "should go beyond canon law" and return the children to their family. Dell'Aqua, however, held the traditional Catholic position: he argued that the Church could not abandon Catholic children. *Le Monde's* publication of Rabbi Zaoui's experience at the Vatican is notable for exposing the Vatican's rigid view regarding the doctrine of Catholic baptism, even in the face of arguments from Jewish religious authorities about the significance of circumcision.

The Grenoble defense committee for the Finaly family, an organization formed to support the interests of the Finaly family, and who often leveraged the press to elevate their communications, addressed the letter from Abbot Deroo that had been published in *Le Monde* on March 10, 1953, with one of their own, which they published on March 19. The defense committee responded to Deroo's arguments about Catholic spirituality taking precedence over Judaism by claiming that such an argument "ignored the laws of Jehovah … the God with whom the Finaly parents marked their alliance with the flesh of their sons." In the article, the committee posed a series of questions, asking "Who now grants nothing to this circumcision? Who has proven intolerance and partisanship? Who only believes in their own God?"[145] In their letter, the committee publicized the view of the Jewish community, which was that the circumcisions of the Finaly brothers confirmed their parents' intent to raise them as Jews. By questioning Deroo and his Church's partisanship and intolerance, the committee deflated the image projected by the Church that they were doing everything they could to return the children. The committee also fought back against Deroo's Catholic exceptionalism and opposed his support of Brun, such as his contention that: "She obeyed her conscience, and she only did her duty."[146] The committee called out his hypocritical usage of the word "conscience, which violated the desires of the children's father and the mother and remained willfully ignorant

about the protracted legal efforts of the family to have them returned."[147]

The response of the Jewish community and its supporters served to dispel rumors,

which supported conservative viewpoints. These included claims that the Finaly parents wanted

their sons to be baptized and raised Catholic and also that the Finaly relatives had not been

actively reclaiming the children. The unity of voices which argued that the circumcision of the

children was proof that the Finaly parents wished for their children to be raised in Judaism is

also notable.

Ritual Abduction and the Church

Historical Precedent

One article in *Le Monde* illustrates how historical precedents of the kidnapping and

forced conversion of Jewish children in Europe related to the Jewish community's anxieties

about the Finaly Affair and how they were portrayed in the press. This article published in *Le

Monde* on March 27, 1953, titled "Two Precedents for the Finaly Affair," was written by an

anonymous member of the clergy. He reminded the newspaper's readership that there was a

history of abduction of Jewish children by the Catholic Church.

The first case he mentioned was the Montel Affair, which occurred in 1840 and involved

a Jewish family from Nîmes. The father, Daniel Montel, was traveling with his pregnant wife

along the Tiber river. They had just made it to their inn when their child, a little girl, was born. A

priest had come to baptize the child, but Daniel Montel refused. A few days later when the

family arrived in Rome, they were surprised to be met with an emissary of the papal

government, several soldiers and a nanny who ordered them to hand their daughter over to their custody. Their justification was that the baby had been baptized and could not remain in the hands of non-Catholics. The father insisted that there had been no baptism, but even so the family was guarded by two sentinels who would protect the baby in the case that her parents tried to abduct her. It was later confirmed that a servant at the Inn where the Montels stayed had baptized the baby girl. Alphonse de Rayneval, chargé d'affaires for the French government, took a special interest in the case and tried to negotiate on behalf of the Montels who were French citizens. The French government threatened to intervene in the situation. This applied pressure to the pope who then agreed to turn the child over to Rayneval only if he raised her in the Catholic faith. The Holy Father would not consent without agreement on this precise condition.[148] The Montel case is comparable to the Finaly Affair in the way that external pressure on the Pope brought forth a level of compromise. In the Finaly Affair, the intense media frenzy led the Pope to approve the return of the children as an effort to not make an already negative public relations situation worse. In either case the compromises had little to do with concern for the child or their family.

The second case cited in the article was the more well-known Mortara Affair. The Finaly Affair was comparable to the Mortara Affair not only because the events were similar, but also because of the media attention that both received. The affair occurred in 1854 in Bologna, a papal state. Three-year-old Edgardo Mortara, son of a Jewish couple, had fallen gravely ill. A Christian servant took it upon herself to secretly baptize Edgardo because she feared he was in mortal danger. Three years later, when the Church learned that Edgardo had been baptized, he was separated from his family and placed in a Catholic school in Rome. Pope Pius IX received the parents and allowed them to see their son but refused to return Edgardo. By 1857, the

Mortara affair began to take "global proportions," with outcries coming from both Europe and America. Edgardo, himself, showed a strong desire to remain Catholic and ended up becoming a Catholic priest. When he turned sixteen the pope addressed him and told Edgardo how dear he was to him. Edgardo was a "very big prize from Christ," which cost the pope "a high price." The pope told Edgardo that because of him there was "a universal outburst against" the apostolic seat. "Governments and peoples, the powers of the world, have declared war to me," stated Pius IX.[149] The pope's comments illustrate the extent to which he was entrenched in Catholic doctrine. To him Edgardo's baptism was a "prize" and a "regeneration" that pleased God. He did not see any moral issues with its administration or treatment of the Mortara parents. Irritated by the deluge of complaints about his handling of the Mortara case, he wondered why this outcry had not arisen in the case of Poland, a country where Catholics were being persecuted. It is apparent that there was something universally appalling about the forced separation of a child from their parents, which rallied governments as well as the public to raise their voices.

These two cases set a precedent for ritual abduction as well as justifiable reasons for Jewish families to be anxious about possible abductions of their children. On June 6, 1953, after the agreed upon deadline for the return of the Finaly children had passed, Chief Rabbi Jacob Kaplan made a statement in his synagogue. After three months the Jewish community had sufficiently proven their "patience and conciliatory spirit." The negotiations, on Kaplan's part, were a way to ensure the return of the children and avoid a deeper rift between Catholics and Jews. At the conclusion of his statement, Kaplan evoked the Mortara Affair and affirmed "that we cannot let the Finaly affair transform into a new Mortara affair." What "was possible a century ago in the papal states, namely, a kidnapping, by the Church, of a young Jewish child who had been secretly baptized, cannot be conceivable in the France of 1953."[150]

Abductions in the Finaly Affair

With the strong historical precedents of cases like the Montel and Mortara affair, it is not surprising that there was anxiety among the Jewish community about the conversion of their children and subsequent abduction. In the Finaly case, the first disappearance of the children occurred after the court of appeals officially designated Hedwig Rosner as the children's legal guardian on June 11, 1952. A few days later, when Moshe Keller, Rosner's representative in Grenoble, and the bailiff went to Brun's home to collect the children, they had disappeared. As already mentioned in the section on *Le Monde*'s coverage of Mother Antonine, a number of women religious, lay people, and clergy were involved in moving the children from Paris to Marseille and finally to Bayonne, where Robert and Gérald attended school until they were abducted again on February 3, 1953. The first abduction was "successful" until late January of 1953 when, per the details of her testimony, Sister Antonine, the Mother Superior of Notre-Dame-de-Sion in Grenoble, learned that the director of the school had disclosed the whereabouts of the children to the prosecutor's office in Bayonne. On February 3, 1953 the children were mysteriously abducted from their school. This was also the day when representatives of their family were scheduled to reclaim them. *Le Monde* featured two initial hypotheses. The first was that the children ran away. But why would they run when their family was coming to collect them? Kidnapping seemed more plausible. *Le Monde* proceeded to report on the suspicious activities of the clergy and Catholic lay people in conjunction with their possible kidnapping.[151] In response, implicated clergy and lay people constructed a wall of silence. Mother Antonine denied responsibility for the February abduction, claiming that she had learned about the disappearance in the newspaper.[152]

In response to the abduction, Hedwig Rosner sent a telegram to the Gard of the seals that was printed in *Le Monde* on February 5, 1953, which implied that religious fanatics were to blame for the children's disappearance. The message also illustrates her hope for French justice:

> Finaly family: whose two children came to be taken in Bayonne, when they were under the hands of justice by religious fanatics, ask for help from the French justice. Denounce the criminal follies of fanatics who want to relight battles both racial and religious. Signed Edwige Rosner-Finaly, Guardian.[153]

At least twelve clergy members were arrested as well as at least five lay people throughout the course of the investigation. The arrested priests, who were referred to collectively as the "Basque priests," received wide support from the Catholic community.

Details about the final abduction reveal the depths to which the clergy went to keep the Finaly children separated from their family. Rumors about their possible location had become a normal occurrence; Brazil, Portugal and Northern Africa had been suggested. Due to the proximity of Bayonne to the border of Spain, many also guessed – correctly – that they may have been smuggled there. On February 24, 1953, *Le Monde* reported the arrests of the priests who had facilitated the children's illegal travel into Spain as well as the mountain guide who led the boys across the Pyrenees.

The children first spent the night in the presbytery of Abbot Ibarburu, priest of Biriatou, a traditional Basque province in southwestern France. To organize the travel, two different abbots, who were later arrested, gave 30,000 Francs ($8500 in 1953) to the mountain guide, Jose Tiomo, otherwise known as Joseph Suspereguy, and 10,000 Francs ($2857 in 1953) to another lay person to outfit the children for the mountain passage. From Suspereguy's testimony, *Le Monde* printed a dramatic account of the boys snowy and dangerous travel over the Pyrenees into Spain entitled "Under the snow to Saint Sebastian." The children rose at dawn on February 13, 1953, to start the mountain passage in the snowstorm. They hiked all day and didn't arrive at their Spanish venta until 11 pm that night.[154] The children would remain hidden in Spain for several months. According to a statement from André Weil of COSOR, the children were also separated from each other while in Spain. Weil remarked that the boys were "separated for far too long during their stay beyond the Pyrenees. In fact, while the eldest was hosted in Guetaria, a small fishing port, Gérald had found hospitality in a mountain village."[155] It is hard to fathom the money spent as well as the danger that the Church put two children through to protect their "Catholic faith." It is distressing that sending two young brothers on a risky illegal journey and then separating them was spiritually motivated.

By sending the children to Spain, the Church also sent them into the "Spain of Franco," as *Esprit* director Albert Bequin eloquently stated. This was a country that would be "very happy to defend the freedom of Christians against the tyranny of Atheist France." Bequin wondered if French clergy responsible for smuggling the children had forgotten this. The *Esprit* director knew that the Church wasn't going to completely modify the norms of canon law because of a few individuals, but also acknowledged that "the Church is not immobile or frozen in this legalism ... the law of the Church like all others, can evolve." Beguin left room for hope of a "coming day when a Finaly affair can no longer emerge."[156]

By February 27, 1953, five Basque priests had been arrested, imprisoned in Bayonne and charged with child abduction and kidnapping.[157] At this time the General Counsel of the Basque country met in Bayonne to discuss the situation. They noted that since the arrests, "emotion has gripped the region" and if nothing was done to support the provisional release of those arrested, "certain politicians," notably Jean Ybarnégaray, a former Vichy minister, would take a violent stance. The counselors declared that "The Basque country recalls where they were during the war and the occupation, despite the risk, it was a place of exile for Israelites, who found the necessary help by the thousands to safeguard their lives." The counselors affirmed their trust in the justice system but considering the "resentment felt and its possible ramifications," they believed that provisional release for those arrested would be the best form of appeasement. Taking into consideration the memories of rescue during the war, there was unanimous support for the motion, which was handed over to the Prefect of the Basse-Pyrénées, Monsieur Delauney. Delauney congratulated the counselors for the moderate terms of their motion, which took the "necessary precautions to maintain order and prevent trouble" and were a departure from the "violent terms of M. Ybarnégaray." The prefectorial authorities reportedly tore up Ybarnégaray's appeals that morning.[158] Despite their position against violent measures and violent people, the counselors were united in their opinion that the priests, who were accused of kidnapping and child abduction deserved provisional release.

Another case, which arose around the same time as the Finaly Affair was "Oradour-sur-Glane." It was not a custody case, but a war-time massacre of civilians in Nazi occupied France, just days after D-Day. A village had been annihilated by Germans, but also by volunteers from Alsace. The verdict in the case was distressing to many, including *Le Monde*, who found the government too lenient. Catherine Poujol has observed that whether intentional or not, *Le Monde* often presented articles about Oradour-sur-Glane and the Finaly Affair on the same page. The German officers were condemned to death, while the Alsatian volunteers and others were condemned to forced labor or imprisonment. An amnesty law made on February 20, 1953, sent all of the implicated Alsatians home.[159] The juxtaposition of the two cases raises the question of whether *Le Monde* and the general public linked the two cases.

On February 27, 1953, *Le Monde* printed an excerpt of an article believed to have been written by Abbot Lanusse-Cazale, former professor of the seminary of Bayonne and colleague of one of the arrested priests. The article was originally printed in two Catholic newspapers, *Éclair Basque* and *Éclair Pyrenees* under the signature "Saint-Vast." The writer directly links the amnesty given to the Alsatians with the arrested priests. Lanusse-Cazale stated "the Finaly children are doing better than the children of Oradour, so keeping them [the priests] in prison is no longer a mistake; it's an error."[160] Although comparing the two events seems oblique, the Oradour-sur-Glane massacre and amnesty for those implicated seemed to have influenced beliefs that those arrested in the Finaly Affair were entitled to provisional release, despite being charged with kidnapping and child abduction. Regardless of the priests actions, which were rooted in Catholic antisemitism, advocates of the priests argued for more lenient sentencing since unlike in the Oradour-sur-Glane case, the priests hadn't been guilty of murder.

On February 28, 1953, *Le Monde* reported that the regional Basque press had called for the liberation of the imprisoned priests. *Le Nouvelle Gazette de Biarritz* wrote that they would protest as long as needed and that "priests who are neither murderers, nor criminals, nor highwaymen, nor thieves" should not be in prison. They declared that their "cry today will be a cry of hope: Free our priests."[161] Abbot Pierre Lafitte, member of the Académie Basque and director of the Basque weekly *Herria*, published a study of Basque law and the Finaly Affair.

Lafitte pointed out that Basque law, did not recognize jurisdiction over the clergy. The clerics

had their own ecclesiastical court, which in cases of conversion would defend the child against

their family. In brief, returning the children to their family before final judgement by the

ecclesiastic court would have been read as an abuse of the right of asylum, in this instance

asylum given to the converted Jewish child from their parents. Lafitte wrote that their "oldest

institutions have been closer to good sense and natural law than many others" and that it was

not surprising that there was nostalgia for it. In conclusion, he remarked that "it pleases us to

admire that, instinctively, the Basque country has reacted in the sense of the old law."[162] There

was historical precedent for the prerogative that the priests were not subject to civil law and

answered to a higher power. It is a complicated argument which projects on to the converted,

children who were not yet at the age of reason, complicity in their conversion and a need for

asylum. The children were treated more as objects and since they were now "saved," they

required protection and defense from the very people who gave them life.

It was a shared opinion in some Catholic circles that the abductors had done their

Christian duty and answered to a higher power. Along these lines, Abbot Idiartegaray, chaplain

of the Maritime Workers in Saint-Jean-de-Luz, wrote a protest letter in the name of the

arrested priests. The abbot justified the actions of the priests on the grounds of conscience. He

declared that "given these circumstances and the formal will of the children," the priests'

attitude was dictated solely by conscious. On the side of justice, Idiartegaray said that they did

not have to comment. They submitted themselves to "a higher jurisdiction." The abbot noted

that it was true, "delivering the children to a representative of the collateral family to take

them to Israel," was the law. "On the other side, he insisted, "is the desire of the children to keep their authentic and sacred rights, remain faithful to their most cherished affections."

Taking a position similar to one that Francois Mauriac had used against Maître Garçon,

Idiartegaray considered the family to be the real abductors of the children stating that their

"protectors allow them to be sacrificed by a legal and undoubtably definite abduction."[163]

Certainly, the Abbot felt there was an unresolvable conflict between matters of "conscious" and

French law. The abbot's scope of conscience was not inclusive of those of other faiths and

beliefs. In the guise of rescue and spiritual saving, was abduction and separation from family

justifiable?

While the press, especially in the Basque region, enabled the propagation of traditional

ideas which supported the baptism, abduction and provisional release of those implicated,

there was an observable outcry from the Jewish and liberal leaning communities which

surfaced in *Le Monde*. On March 7, 1953, Baron Guy de Rothschild, who served as the President

of the Central Consistory, made a statement indicating that they hoped for appeasement and

supported Chief Rabbi Kaplan in his work to achieve an agreement. Rothschild made it clear

that the rabbinate of France was "not going to confirm a forced conversion or the forfeiture of

a family's rights. After dispelling the myth of ritual murder, we scarcely appreciate the reality of

ritual abduction."[164] By "ritual murder," Rothschild is referring to the blood libel which first

circulated in the 12th century in "The Accusation of the Ritual Murder of St. William of

Norwich," written by Thomas of Monmouth. According to this libel, Jews would ritually kill a

Christian child and drain him of blood. According to the account, "the Jews, without the

shedding of human blood, could neither obtain their freedom, nor could they ever return to

their fatherland."[165] This false narrative would arise over and over again throughout history and serve as a catalyst for antisemitism. Much effort, as inferred by Rothschild, had been made to dispel the lies of ritual murder over the years. What was even worse was the very real ritual abduction of Robert and Gérald Finaly.

In addition, Rothschild, along with other Jewish individuals and organizations, made statements in the press with regard to the reprehensible act of abduction. The World Jewish Congress in New York, also used the term "ritual abduction" in a statement made to the Associated Press on March 23, 1953, and considered the affair "an affront with respect to the humanity of Jews around the world."[166] Rabbi Jais, in his emotional response to Abbot Deroo's views that the rights of God should be considered in the case of the Finaly brothers, directly reproached the Church for abducting the children. Jais referred to snatching children from their legitimate family, violating their souls, sequestering them and then expatriating them. It was as if they were "erased from the world of the living for their loved ones." Jais asked if this was not the "most egregious crime?," and criticized Deroo's view that "all these offenses were not only lawful but also 'divinely' good.[167] France's intellectuals also released a statement regarding the Finaly Affair in which they wondered "how there could be a question in our country and in our time of a physical right of the Church over baptized children." They judged it "regrettable" that doctrine is reliant on "higher spiritual realities but ends up justifying acts ... as reprehensible from the standpoint of simple morality as the concerted abduction of children."[168] This group's belief in civil law stood in opposition to those who supported the Basque priests.

Rabbi Jacob Kaplan raised the issue of abduction in his emotional statement, published on June 6, 1953, after the agreed upon deadline for the return of the children had passed. Kaplan condemned the Church for keeping the children in Spain and faulted the ecclesiastical hierarchy for never officially condemning the kidnappers and their accomplices. Kaplan

observed that "Catholic theologians have been able to support, without censure, the canonical

legitimacy of this ritual kidnapping." This is a valid concern as illustrated in the platform

provided by *Le Monde* to figures like Abbot Deroo, François Mauriac, Abbot Lanusse-Cazale and

Abbot Idiartegaray. Also relevant, Kaplan appealed to Jewish parents very directly, warning

them that "no Jewish child is safe from a secretly administered baptism; no Jewish child, even if

improperly baptized, is protected against the fanatical zeal of priests who take them from their

families to keep them in the Catholic faith."[169]

André Weil, Treasurer of COSOR and a key player in the negotiations for the children's

return, made a statement in support of Rabbi Kaplan on June 7, 1953. In this published

declaration, Weil called for "the spiritual condemnation" of the priests as well as the

newspapers which had supported that the baptism had justified the abduction. He objected to

the fact that those responsible for the abduction were not behind bars and condemned. After

being patient and silent for three months, they are no longer hopeful. In conclusion, Weil had

four guesses as to the location of the children:

> Either they are in the hands of the Catholic Church; or they are in the hands of a gang that will blackmail us by revealing themselves shortly; or they are in the hands of the network that had taken them to the Basque Country; or one of the children is no longer alive, and then they would want to hide the truth.[170]

This section has illustrated some key debates particular to the abduction of Robert and

Gérald Finaly. Those who supported the Basque priests and may have recalled their history of

saving lives during the occupation, argued for more lenient treatment of the priests in the form

of provisional release. They also espoused the belief that the actions of the implicated clergy

were motivated by conscious and should be judged by a higher power. There was little acknowledgment or care that through their reprehensible acts, which were justified by Catholic

doctrine, that they had broken civil law. Those on the opposite side of the spectrum had more

hope in the justice system. They believed that those implicated should be locked up for their

crimes and that the Church should publicly reprimand them. There was a criticism that the

press had given too much of a platform to those who supported the Finaly baptism and

subsequent abductions.

Negotiation

As the Finaly Affair progressed, there was talk about possible negotiations or

appeasement measures created to bring the children home. There were two sets of

negotiations in the affair. The Vatican entrusted Cardinal Gerlier, the Archbishop of Lyon with

representing the Church and negotiating directly with the family, the Central Consistory and

COSOR. This negotiation led up to the agreement of March 6. There was an agreed upon silence

between all parties at the request of the Church. The silence was broken when Rabbi Kaplan

made a frustrated and emotional statement on June 6, 1953, on the grounds that the Finaly

children were not returned by the deadline. Archival evidence also shows that once the media

frenzy started to become a public relations issue, around January 1953, a proposal also began

to be worked out at the Vatican. The Vatican negotiations were also protected by a veil of

silence.

Silence and rumor seem to have a symbiotic relationship. The rumors were more supportive

of the conservative Catholic prerogative, which included the support of amnesty for those

imprisoned, ensuring that the children would remain in France and be able to continue

practicing Catholicism. An early rumor reported by *Le Monde*'s correspondent in Biarritz on

February 27, 1953, mentioned a possible deal between French and Spanish authorities for the children's return in exchange for the freedom of the imprisoned priests.[171] One of the more outlandish reports came from *Herria*, a Basque publication. On June 20, 1953, it indicated three points of an agreement made between Hedwig Rosner, André Weil and Rabbi Jacob Kaplan and was signed by Abbot Lafitte:

1. The children will be raised in France
2. The children will not be cut from all Christian influence
3. The children will be able to correspond with the one who saved them from death.

In actuality; Kaplan, Rosner and Weil did not agree to these points.[172] The conditions were also exceedingly favorable to the conservative Catholic position on the affair.

The official negotiation between the family, Rabbi Kaplan, the Church and COSOR began on February 18, 1953, when Kaplan learned from André Weil that Father Pierre Chaillet, a priest who was known to have saved many Jews during the war, wanted to see him. Chaillet represented Cardinal Gerlier and wished to propose an agreement for the return of the children. Pertaining to the request of the Church to negotiate, Kaplan, in his memoir, stated that he felt that such a project would be favorable, but he had some conditions. First, the children should be returned to Hedwig Rosner as soon as the court made its decision. Second, there should not be any influence of the Church in the children's education. Third, there should not be a condition that the children remain in France until adulthood. The last condition was that after the Court of Cassation decided on the case, Hedwig Rosner could take the children where she wished. On the side of the Catholic Church, Father Chaillet requested that all of the legal complaints against those implicated in the case be removed. Kaplan felt this would work as long as the children were returned. The family opted to negotiate out of hope that it would bring the quick return of the children. The Church recommended that once the children were returned, Rosner could stay with them at a COSOR establishment, which would be religiously

neutral. André Weil offered his home outside of Paris.[173]

After Rabbi Kaplan's accusatory statement of June 6, the Church attempted to defend

itself. On the following news day, Father Chaillet provided a statement as well as the text of the

March 6th agreement. In his statement, Chaillet commented on the doubt that Rabbi Kaplan

placed on the Catholic hierarchy who were part of the negotiation. His solution was to disclose

the terms of the agreement and detail the steps that had been taken over the past three

months in Spain. He explained the role of Germaine Ribière, who was selected to be Cardinal

Gerlier's representative to both the civil and religious authorities in Spain. Chaillet detailed the

numerous efforts Ribière had made to facilitate the return of the children.[174]

Before looking at the terms of the agreement, it is valuable to understand Rabbi Jacob

Kaplan's perspective on the negotiation. Kaplan explained his reasoning to two journalists in

this way: "with the agreement, we have some chance of having the children; without the

agreement, we will win the lawsuit, but the children stay in Spain."[175] Kaplan legitimately felt

than negotiation was the only way to secure the return of the children, which explains why

some of the conditions, particularly the first condition was more favorable to the Church. It

indicated that once the children returned all that was "said or published in these agonizing

emotional events" would be forgotten and joint efforts would be made to end all criminal

proceedings. It was also decided upon that when the children were brought back to France,

Rosner and the children would live on the property of André Weil in Saint Leonard near Paris. A

social worker would also be selected by Rosner, Kaplan and the Catholic authorities to look

after the morale and health of the children. During their stay in Saint Leonard, all decision making concerning the children would be collectively made by the three parties. It was also determined that no religious pressure would be exerted on the children. There would also be a maximum delay of four months to reach the conclusion of the affair.[176]

As the media frenzy heightened, Catholic officials became increasingly anxious. The Congregation of the Holy Office, the Vatican authority on Church doctrine, began to work on a proposal for the return of the Finaly children. The proposal included the condition that the boys be placed in a neutral educational institution, and similar to the March 6th agreement, guaranteed amnesty for Antoinette Brun, Mother Antonine and others who had been implicated in the scandal. A clause was also included that the agreement would ensure that the boys could continue their Catholic education.[177] The pope did not approve the agreement immediately and instead gave the responsibility of resolving the situation to Cardinal Gerlier. After learning that Gerlier could get no further concessions from the Jewish side and in consideration of the media frenzy, the pope relented and approved the proposal. On March 23, 1953, the Vatican sent the Nuncio in Madrid news of the approval and instructions to find and return the children.[178] It took approximately three months after the approval for Robert and Gérald Finaly to return to France. Because of the silence, which concealed the pope's personal involvement in the approval, the Spanish clergy took their time producing the children.

On June 27, 1953, Father Chaillet announced that the agreement of March 6 had finally succeeded. Chaillet indicated that they would start the process to return the children with the Spanish Civil authorities in Saint Sebastian.[179] Soon after, the Finaly Children arrived in Saint Leonard. On July 25, 1953, Hedwig Rosner sent a registered letter to her lawyer with instructions to withdraw all of her legal complaints against those implicated in the scandal. She specified that she had removed all of the complaints filed against all parties, religious and lay, even though certain figures on the Catholic side asked her to maintain them for certain lay individuals. Rosner also stated that the withdrawal was not meant as a disavowal of any of her supporters or representatives. Even though the withdrawal was a condition of the March 6 agreement, she claimed that her action "should not be considered as the execution of any clause of the agreement reached on March 6, 1953, which became null and void in its entirety." It had always been her intention to withdraw her complaints and "contribute to the maintenance of public peace as much as possible, so violently disturbed by an affair that I had never wished for or foreseen." Rosner considered the event a "triumph of public opinion and French justice" and expressed her gratitude to both.[180]

The negotiation, to Chief Rabbi Kaplan, represented the course needed to obtain the return of the children. It was apparent to him that without some negotiation with the Church, the family might win the civil case, but the children would most likely remain in Catholic custody. We can infer from his viewpoint that Kaplan himself did not trust the Church to return the children on their own initiative. The Church's initiation of the negotiations, was less a statement of their willingness to return Robert and Gérald, but an effort to control the discussion and ensure that their conditions were met. The public relations nightmare, which was impacting the Church, was also a strong motivator to negotiate. The withdrawal of all legal complaints by Hedwig Rosner in July of 1953, was an example of the family's ability to remain above the fray. Claiming it was always her intention to drop the charges, Rosner handled the situation with grace and an eye toward peace. As a parent, she probably also wanted to move on with her life and focus on helping Robert and Gérald transition to their new lives in Israel.

Conclusion

The return of Robert and Gérald Finaly made international news. On June 27, 1953, *The New York Times* commented that "the two Jewish war orphans … have been the innocent centers of the worst religious storm of post-war France."[181] This reporting shows how, in the overall crisis of Jewish war orphans, children were understood to serve as objects in a wider debate about the relationship between Judaism and Christianity.

This thesis has shown that the newspaper coverage of the Finaly Affair was a key element in perpetuating both antisemitism stemming from the Catholic Church and its doctrine, as well as early post-war references to the Holocaust. In covering the guardianship, baptism and abductions of Robert and Gérald Finaly, the press provided the Church and its supporters with a platform to promote ideas rooted in historic antisemitism with little to no reproach. There was wide support, especially from the Basque region of France, for the baptism and subsequent abduction of the children. These ideas included Christian supersessionism, which served as a justification for converting Jewish children and contributed to an erasure of Jewish culture. Specific to baptism, we explored the range of opinions regarding the validity of the Finaly baptism and whether the Church's strict adherence to doctrine remained relevant. One of the most unsettling ideas, separating converted children from all Jewish influence and their families, originated directly from Catholic doctrine which historically justified child abductions. A common theme in the debate was the authority of divine law versus French civil law. While the Finaly family and those with more secular views put their faith in the justice process, clergy members argued that the issues presented in the Finaly Affair demanded the authority of higher spiritual powers.

Although *Le Monde* and other newspapers provided a convenient platform for conservative voices that put the Jewish community on the defensive, it also allowed Jews and others to begin to express their feelings about the events of the Holocaust and to clearly state the extent of Jewish loss. Contrary to what many have claimed regarding silence surrounding the Holocaust in these early years, coverage of the Finaly Affair in *Le Monde* has shown that Jews were not silent about the events and suffering they experienced during the Holocaust when declaring their positions on the case. The representation of Antoinette Brun in the press shows how gendered portrayals of her as a saint, a conniver or "old fool," depending on the journalist or publication, contributed to the perpetuation of negative stereotypes about Jews. Brun was deceptive and manipulated both the legal process and her own self-portrayal, which ranged from hero to martyr depending on her audience. She was overtly antisemitic to the Finaly relatives and was happy to separate Robert and Gérald from all Jewish influence so that they could be raised as "good and true Frenchmen."[182] Her act of saving the children and refusing to return them to their families crystallized a new post-war form of antisemitism in which religious justifications became an acceptable mask for the perpetuation of age-old Christian prejudices against Judaism.

After finally reuniting with the children, Hedwig Rosner told the press that her intention was to bring the boys to Israel, but not immediately. "An attack has been committed against their conscience; we do not want to commit a second. They will live with their family, and I fully realize that adapting to this new environment will take some time."[183] On July 25, 1953, the children flew to Israel with their Aunt Hedwig. Robert was 12 years old and Gérald had recently turned 11 in June. Robert and Gérald Finaly faced challenging circumstances in their new home.

For example, they had grown up speaking French, but their Aunt Hedwig spoke only German and Hebrew. The young Finalys spent their first night in Israel at a kibbutz founded by members of the French resistance called Neve Ilan. It was nicknamed the "Little France in Israel." At the kibbutz, the children were welcomed by French speaking children their age. The atmosphere was much calmer at Neve Ilan compared to Europe. The kibbutz held a reception for the children which included Rosner and the Jewish social worker who came from Paris. Robert and Gérald also began to learn Hebrew.

Unsurprisingly, coverage of their new life in Israel in *Le Monde* included details intended to soften the blow to the Church that their departure represented. An article of July 28, 1953, reassured its readership that the kibbutz was visited regularly by French priests and tourists who aided in the children's adjustment to life in Israel. It also reassured its Catholic readership that, two French churches stood in close proximity to the kibbutz, should the children be interested in visiting them. At its conclusion, the article cited the Rosners' desire to step out of the public eye, for the sake of the boys.[184] And over time, Robert and Gérald transitioned successfully, learned Hebrew and continue to enjoy their lives in Israel.[185]

Judeo-Catholic Dialogue: The Way Forward

Maurice-Ruben Hayoun, in his preface to Rabbi Jacob Kaplan's memoir, *l'Affaire Finaly*, argues that the Finaly Affair marked a turning point in both the history of French Judaism and Judeo-Christian relations.[186] While Rabbi Kaplan's statement of June 6 evoked a vehement response from many Catholics, Kaplan also acknowledged that at the same time members of the French Catholic Church began to hold a new position on the doctrine of baptism. He stated that the French religious hierarchy no longer accepted the historical Catholic doctrine which dictated that Jewish children who were baptized against the will of their parents could not be returned to their families.[187] Priscilla Dale Jones points to Catholic clergy such as Father Riquet who suggested that Church doctrine had become outmoded.[188] Perhaps Riquet was among the clergy that were no longer accepting of the Church's rigid adherence to doctrine. The anonymous Catholic whose statement was published in *Le Monde*, himself a common Catholic, questioned the logic of such strict adherence to the doctrine of baptism, while at the same time, the Church allowed for more flexibility with the doctrine on marriage.[189] Perhaps the time had come to reevaluate Catholic doctrine? Rabbi Kaplan reminds us, in his memoir, that the fact that Church did restitute the Finaly brothers to their Jewish family should not be minimized. With this act they "annulled the dramatic precedent of the Mortara Affair." Kaplan went on to express that "The happy resolution of the Finaly Affair now makes it impossible for any repetition of such a case."[190]

Unlike today, in 1953, there was no suggestion on the part of the Catholic Church of a parallel route to salvation in non-Christian religions.[191] In 1965, the *Declaration on the Relations of the Church to Non-Christian Religions*, more commonly known as *Nostra Aetate,* was the first Church declaration considering the validity of non-Christian religions. It was initiated by Pope Paul VI and recognized the shared "spiritual patrimony common to Christians and Jews" and promoted fraternal dialogue between the two faiths. Importantly, *Nostra Aetate* retracted the charge that it was "the Jews" who killed Jesus, which historically fueled antisemitism and Jewish persecution, a sentiment which influenced the actors in the Finaly Affair. The declaration denounced "hatred, persecutions, displays of antisemitism, directed against Jews at any time by anyone."[192] *Nostra Aetate* marked the beginning of an effort, on the part of the Catholic Church, to reckon with its uncomfortable past concerning the Jews.

The progress of Judeo-Catholic relations and the Finaly Affair's influence on it provides a conceivable subject for future research. There was a need, in the post-war era, for the missionary perspective of the Catholic Church to be reevaluated. One change that was made was the separation of the Catholic Church's missionary operations from their approach to the Jews. These structural changes illustrate that the Catholic Church moved away from including Jews in their missionary objectives. The new focus moved to dialogue as well as reparative language, which previously had shown contempt for the Jews and their faith. Other political events led the Church to reconsider its own imperialism. Not only had it proselytized Jews, but the Church was also responsible for the conversion and cultural erasure of indigenous and other non-Catholic peoples as part of what was believed to be God's providential design. A purposeful move toward respectful dialogue and understanding will hopefully help unite Jews and Catholics through conversation and cooperation.[193]

9 785786 787581